Whispers Of A Butterfly Warrior

Healing & Recovery on Damascus Road

PATRICIA HAWKINSON

authorHOUSE®

AuthorHouse™
1663 Liberty Drive
Bloomington, IN 47403
www.authorhouse.com
Phone: 1-800-839-8640

First published by AuthorHouse   9/29/2010

ISBN: 978-1-4389-9193-1 (sc)

Library of Congress Control Number: 2010913653

Printed in the United States of America
Bloomington, Indiana

This book is printed on acid-free paper.

Dedication

This Book is dedicated to all those souls that are struggling to find an inner peace in a world of darkness. People seeking spirituality or change, those who have knowledge of religious beliefs but waver with weakness due to status, circumstance, loss, self image or pain that prevents them from searching. Too many times a person is provoked to fail again when on a verge of breakthrough to greater things in life. After you experience life altering events that shatter all faith and hope the spirit grows weary in any attempts to find or strive to greatness. Sometimes it takes a blinding light that makes us stop, listen and absorb truth. We all have a different magnitude of this light and sometimes see it over and over again on our journey. The light is usually found in the darkest part of our life while at a crossroads and our decisions to ignore it or embrace it shall shape us into our future. Transformation often requires a fierce and forceful impact that reaches deep into our senses to be effective. On a road less traveled such as Damascus Road where Paul became Saul in the Bible, he encountered a light that made him blind for three days. We as people are searching for the bolt of lightning that can alter our lives, but many of us think we are beyond its reach. This Collection of poems will wind you down a mountain of despair and take you to a deep valley of pain where you can experience the raw imagery of struggle, knowing you are not alone. Every piece of work was written so that you can fully view the beauty in the lightning no matter where on the road you are positioned. Broken Concrete, graveled dirt, muddy trails, blackened alleys and one way streets will all lead you back to the same intersection where the light shines. We can use many streets to get to our destination but Damascus Road is the only one where heaven scorches us with a light that is so blinding that it can make us see the truth. These poetic stories breathe life into whatever obstacle has betrayed your soul, buried your heart and injured your spirit. Journey with me to where trouble and chaos are met, by the mighty hand of GOD. ....and Butterfly Warriors are born to whisper… The Butterfly Warrior is a metaphor, it is a term best used to describe transformation or drastic change such as when a fury caterpillar is liquefied to become a soft butterfly. The Warrior of a butterfly is the core strength or force within such a fragile creature that helps it evolve under such amazing circumstances that provides the recovery needed to change The history of the Butterfly Warrior is described by Aztec Legends as a Mother Goddess . She re-birthed soldiers or warriors who died in the battle for good and women who died in childbirth by transforming their core soul back to life in a different form. It is believed they were reincarnated back to our earthly realm as butterflies, some legends say they become the stars in the night skies. In this Aztec myth the metaphor of coming back to earth to finish a mission of our soul and aspire a higher elevation between people that manifests peace and harmony .Imminent to our spiritual survival ,today's society we have people who act in the capacity of the Aztec legend everyday by bringing back to life the faith, hope and aspirations in others and show us that we are powerful and can move beyond any obstacle of hurt or pain. A group of major Self help leaders, spiritual teachers and writers who fight against social injustice, teach personal growth to people who are lost in abuse, addictions, bad mindsets and destructive life paths. These Warriors of today have started a global movement in the 21st century to help individuals to find responsibility, take ownership of actions that divinely affect themselves and others in this world. A Butterfly Warrior is an activist that is motivated by peace and love to see the greater possibility in people with harmony that respectfully elevates each others. A shift happens when we learn that we are an energy created by GOD to do great things, to be his helping hands, inspiring words and mercy for those who are afflicted by the destructive road of darkness. Elevation of our higher calling to make this world transform by our actions ,speech, love and generosity makes each one of us realize that we are all a piece of a beautiful mosaic painting made by GOD. The picture is pivotal to all mankind and we are all import to the production of positive and negative energy that creates mankind. It. My journey may have great meaning to me but it must be used as a stepping stone for others to find their wings with a bit of comfort. Many butterfly Warriors will find something that sparks the necessary desire to be liquefied and changed. The poems on the pages of this book were birthed in tears built in turmoil and blossomed by determination that cannot be conformed or defined but chosen by a person. We live surrounded by obstacles that can either be the saddest default that keeps us the same or the greatest triumphs that lead us to learn how to fly . A warrior never fears only defends and protects while willing to die for others .A butterfly glides like the wind and is defined by its unique colors and soft texture. Every creature great and small was crafted by GOD's hand to be both strength and compassion and that is the way I define a butterfly warrior,

" A word fitly spoken is like apples of gold in settings of silver"

Proverbs 25:11(NKJV)

Table of Contents

Chapter 1   Educated On A Road Of Darkness   1

Chapter 2   Climbing A Bridge To Change   25

Chapter 3   Redemption In The Street   61

Chapter 4   Concrete Ashes from a Blinding light   89

Chapter One:

Educated On A Road Of Darkness

The world and people shape our views at an early age .We are defined by everything from status and money to our body shape or beautiful face. Society educates us in every form but our heart, soul and spirit. Our mind can either accept the distorted version of what we are taught in the darkness that we have been born in or we can stretch to find the road of change. There is no person beyond GOD's reach and no soul too lost to be found and there is definitely no road too far away or sin too foul that can keep us in the darkness. The first step out of the black cloud surrounding our vision is realizing that we have choices. We are taught to hate ourselves if we do not achieve what others do, to compare success of a person by the type of car they drive or cost of the home they live in. Greed and envy, materialism or popularity among people and the ability to see how these things destroy the human spirit more than uplift it is the compromise that has stolen the true education of our heart. To recognize the destruction surrounding us gives us the ability to enlighten our souls. The education of darkness and the roads that I chose in my past brought people to me that gave me clarity. Preachers, gangbangers, inmates ,successful businessmen, drug addicts, alcoholics, housewives and average American people I encountered all shared the same common thread that gave me the stories to show you how the education of darkness is our deepest problem. Walk thru the darkness with me to feel the stories that remind you we are bonded together on the journey and united we can lighten the road.

Proverbs 3:5-6
Trust in the LORD with all your heart and lean not on your own understanding; in all your ways acknowledge him, and he will make your paths straight.

Educated On Road of Darkness

We are made from his rib, created by his dust and cut from the very same cloth….
Educated on a road of Darkness only the Cardinal Sins of our destruction are taught,
Greed & Pride, to love & Lust materialism, Wrath, Envy gluttony and sloth
Educated on a road of Darkness only the Cardinal Sins of our destruction are taught

Destiny is not found at the bottom of a shot glass, Strength is not in a bottle of wine
If you spend more time with a beer than a bible then you must think you have more time
Greatness is not in the car you drive and Achievement is not the Clubs VIP all access line
Make choices of your character carefully because life does not allow you to press rewind.

Your promotion and raise was honored on earth but what was the price you paid?
Did you forfeit love bonds, family and friends to get the dream house where you laid
Was it worth all the people you hurt or crushed to become the rich man so self-made
And the bad habits you picked up along the way that you eloquently sniff off a blade

We are made from his rib, created by his dust and cut from the very same cloth….
Educated on a road of Darkness only the Cardinal Sins of our destruction are taught,
Greed & Pride, to Love & Lust materialism, Wrath, Envy gluttony and sloth
Educated on a road of Darkness only the Cardinal Sins of our destruction are taught

If love is not enough and you need to cheat and disrespect a marriage or your home
It is because you never knew a higher power of GOD that never leaves you all alone
If you need the bar friends, play pretend to have a friend then you have not yet grown
And if you need that high, accept the lie because fear to fly is all you have ever known…

Potential is not in a pipe, Success is not in a Master card Visa or High Credit Score
Respect is not to the man who won but to the man who worked and endured….
Dirty deeds don't get redeemed in you unless you repent to a heart that is pure
And some of the most admired beautiful people are plainly a self seeking whore

We are made from his rib, created by his dust and cut from the very same cloth….
Educated on a road of Darkness only the Cardinal Sins of our destruction are taught,
Greed & Pride, to love & Lust materialism, Wrath, Envy gluttony and sloth
Educated on a road of Darkness only the Cardinal Sins of our destruction are taught

AWAKE

I am ebony and I am also Ivory.....
I am the thorn on a rose, I am twining ivy,
I am the winds soft wisp, frost that is glistening,
the burden that is lifting and the tornadoes fury fisting,
I am the moisture you feel misting, an earthquake line shifting,
I am the core of the Earth, hearing every word and listening.

I am the hatred blooming, your unexplained dooming,
the stock market zooming and the violent fear looming,
I am toxic gases fuming ,terrorist bombs that are booming,
the gun clicking and wounding, I am killing those doing,
serving you the piece of American pie you chose to be chewing.

I am the homeless bum that you don't know is alive,
I am the success of your morally unbalanced ego strive,
I am the creed that you forgot and mistakes you must repeat,
I am the bad memories of your life you wish you could delete,
I am the return of a seed you sewed, that made God weep.

I am the choice you are not making and the lack of will,
I am the bottom of the road when your over the hill,
I am the call you didn't make, the promise you did break,
I am acceptance of the problem by ignoring what you make,
I am the compromise of ethics that makes you all so fake,
I am the world you chose because of what you create,
I am the coma of society sleeping, that someday must AWAKE!

**1 Thessolonians 4:13 But I would not have you to be ignorant, brethren, concerning them which are asleep, that ye sorrow not, even as others which have no hope.
"A man is a product of his thoughts .What he thinks, he becomes"......MOHANDAS KARAMCHAND GANDHI 1869-1948**

We The People

The twin towers have fallen and will never be forgotten….
Many hearts are buried in the ash and souls lay beneath the bottom
They say Gods face was seen in the clouds of smoke that exhaled,
But his soul was given to the people when his palm was nailed.

Columbine students ran from bullets on an ordinary school day….
Yes we remember to stop for coffee but take no time to pray.
We the people watch these stories like they are a story someone wrote.
This is your America , use your power to speak and your right to vote.

Oklahoma City Bombing, Why did so many have to die?
Another school shooting- a child gunmen and bullets fly…
Long Island sound, late evening and a plane lights up the sky….
Midwest in springtime, Red River North brings floods record high.

Homes are destroyed by tornados crops dry out from heat…
Ozone layers, peel away as we pollute the livestock we eat.
We create more chemicals, products and inventions of tomorrow..
We set trends and examples that we want people to follow.
We the people spend no time solving the problems but adding to the sorrow.

We invent machines that will allow the dead to still live.
We believe we control and choose when a body will give.
We create medicines that are deadlier than the disease.
We dump toxic waste and material in our ocean and seas,
And we destruct our next breath toward death with such ease.

Addictions were advertised, created and well designed.
Manufacturers thought of our health and then made it resign.
Fourteen Million Americans are alcoholic and we create new wine.
Because the American Government will do anything to make a dime,
And we the people believe that the problems not mine.

Revelation 21:8
**But the fearful, and unbelieving, and the abominable, and murderers, and
whoremongers, and sorcerers, and idolaters, and all liars, shall have their part in the lake
which burneth with fire and brimstone: which is the second death.**

Learned

When A gun was put in my face, I felt the meaning in fear.
When I watched my friend die, I knew why I was put here.
When a broken bottle was put to my neck and my kid called a nigger,
I learned the meaning of not reacting, how it made me bigger.
When I was raped the first time, I understood the desire to kill,
The second time I understood how revenge is at God's will.
When I was strapped down to a table, in a room with no view,
I found the meaning of freedom, only lives inside of you.
When I saw a friend loose all the feeling in his body whole,
Paralyzed , he made me look past his body and into his soul.
When I became homeless, had no money, food or place to sleep,
I learned to be thankful for every piece of food that I eat.
When I was lied, cheated and mentally abused by a person I trust,
I learned horrible things make us humble and sometime are a must!
When someone I loved, cut a woman to pieces in a violent rage,
I learned why people don't read the book but just the last page.
When a friend put a 12 gage in his mouth and blasted his own brain,
I learned there are so many silent people living with so much pain.
When a molested teenager found courage to speak from poems I wrote,
I learned that God was using me as a vessel even though I felt useless & broke.
I learned of addiction thru a pipe that showed me the devil was real.
When I rehabilitated I learned how Gods' love and grace heal.
I learned there was great power in written or spoken word,
Because I had prayed to God and the heavens had heard...

1 PETER 5:8 **Be sober, be vigilant; because your adversary the devil, as a roaring lion, walketh about, seeking whom he may devour:**
Psalm 34:17 **The righteous cry, and the LORD heareth, and delivereth them out of all their troubles.**
PSALM 56:3 **When I am afraid, I will trust You. I praise GOD for his word. I trust GOD, so I am not afraid. What can human beings do to me?**

Censorship America

You cannot keep me quiet, I am the 1st Amendment and I have a voice,
I am a parent, blue collar worker and registered voter to make a choice.

I am CNN showing you censored pictures of victims because your mind is fragile.
So we won't put the real image of homeless hurricane victims as helpless as a child.

We sensationalize scandals and a politician who cheats on his dying wife....
But only give 30 seconds to a hero that stood for something and gave his life.

We say gas prices cannot be contained unless in state of emergency, then it is gouging,
And the governor is to busy having a mental day at his beach house poolside lounging.

You cannot censor raw reality when it lands in our driveway with a foreclosure sign,
And you forgot to show that there wasn't enough food for those on the charity kitchen line.

You cannot quiet hunger while you spend millions on a political campaign....
That shows me that your only interests are for self and your shallowness is vain.

You cannot quiet or censor the American people that give their lives for you in Iraq,
And when they come back with Post Traumatic Stress then nobody has their back?

People leave their jobs and 20 year careers now amount to a little brown box,
An again your told by CNN that the economy is ok and don't worry about your stocks.

Censorship, hiding what is right and making us slowly agree to societies decay....
Aren't you sick of seeing it get worse as the news tells you it will all be ok?

When will the censorship stop, can we wait for ethnic cleansing and curfews,
Or do we the people who believe in the 1st Amendment stand up and say our views.

American Censorship has gone too far when it tells you the war is ending.....
Because those guys that are dying every day are not acting or pretending.

Censorship in America can keep you hopeful and blinded into believing...
Yet everyday another job is lost, home gone and family is left grieving.

BLACKOUT.....

"say no to drugs campaign poem"

A Saturday night ….she drops some X and takes a quick hit of acid.
A couple of beers later and suddenly she is beyond plastered…
The house party is jumping, the music still going strong
She doesn't care about anything ….but that feeling to belong.
She is your church going kid, the quiet neighbor next door….
But tonight she is anything and everything they want in a druggie whore.
She thinks drugs make her yet they are only the make of her need..
Her need for love and attention create her in a way that projects a sleeze.
She feels so good, so damn high right now, don't want come down…
Don't want to jones, resorting to beg on her knees from the ground…
The addiction, drug switching to stop twitching just for a chemical tease.
Such the overwhelming feeling when there is not enough to please.
She is the greatest actress as she is playing off the withdrawl so cool.
Drunker and drunker she gets to fill the void, as she mumbles like a fool.
It is about five am and coming down takes a toll making her feel tired…
Her body is still tingling from the numbness of a night of being wired.
Her lips white with resin, cracked, dry swollen and stinging sore….
The reflection of herself in the mirror is unkind but she is wanting more.
She tokes the smoke, a little more hydroponic-chronic, just some pot….
She feels wet and hot, body sweaty from that little crack-cocaine rock…
Her body convulses, limbs itching repulses as she lay in the bed…
Comatosed in a blackout of overdose, about to die, wishing she were dead.
Felt the need for drugs to feel ecstasy, adored, loved, accepted and why?
Because society could not teach us to say no, it is a common tragic way to die.

20 percent of adults in America use some form of illegal drugs on a daily or monthly basis and have dependency or addiction and over 30 percent of teens age 11 and above are using drugs on a regular or frequent basis…….14 million Americans are currently alcoholics in recovery, relapse or denial.

EVERY SIX MINUTES.....

I can remember that man's face and the smell of his cologne…
I can remember that smell of the leather interior on the ride home.
I can remember his words of how he told me I should do as he said…..
Or I could just be left there in Compton and maybe found dead.
It was a late night in Los Angeles and many bottles of cognac gone…
The Porsche was waxed like silk and the radio played my favorite song,
Little did I know that the roses had thorns that would injure me like a fawn…
And my night of terror was moments away and would last until the dawn.
I can remember my mind going to a place that brought me to a daze…
But the picture of his face is a memory that I can never faze…
Only to be reminded how the minds memory sometimes replays
Cold moving like the rain but strong like the sun's very ray….
I saw his hand on my throat, his fist cracking on my jaw…
I heard him say don't scream as I struggled for the door…
His hands tore my clothes and I kept screaming "No More"
He said "you all say that bitch but you know you love it whore"
I scratched, I punched, I kicked bit him and screamed….
Terrified I gave up and pretended it was all a bad dream
He was one of those nice guys or at first it did seem….
Little did I know the monster inside that was so very mean.
I cried thru every minute as my head hit the wall….
He laughed at my terror, asking who was I going to call…
Rape is an act of violence and people treat it very small…
And women face these acts that are veiled by society like a shall.
Ignorance to hide that women experience this deviation….
And that an act of violence is labeled as a man's sexual creation
Is to say that these are fairytales of women or artistic imagination,
Yet, Every six minutes a women is violently raped in this Nation.

Statistics show 1 in every 5 children are raped or molested and a women is raped every 6 minutes in America … I in 3 women are either sexually or physically abused in their lifetime. Stop Sexual Violence it is a crime not a pleasure.

Psalm 23:4 Even if I walk through a very dark valley, I will not be afraid, because you are with me. Your rod and walking stick comfort me.

His Words My Wounds

My mom had started asking, why is it that I never would finish my plate
I think of that man I loved and how he had taught me my own self hate.
How he had said that I was not his type and "the biggest girl" that he ever did date
His words were an exchange that disempowered me and made me change my fate
And that is why I would vomit every time I left the table after I had just ate….
I was big but I was told I was beautiful from every man that I ever knew
So his words that fat was ugly made me feel as if my weight made me ugly too
And then every magazine said that your body was your beauty so it must be so true
And every woman with smaller curves than me made me think I want to be thinner too.
When he said that I allowed myself to be unattractive after baby weight gain….
And said that it was his excuse to cheat on me with a woman of a smaller frame,
I felt like I was not pretty enough, he was repulsed by me and the weight I didn't tame
And every time he cheated or lied made me feel more helpless and to blame.
Then he said his friends were shocked that he dated someone as BIG as me…
And now I felt like they were laughing at him because I was not acceptable beauty
So I starved myself to death, so my fat would be something you could no longer see
To become a model image he liked, I vomited till it hurt so that I could be set free.
I feel sick when I eat, Disgusted at myself, I sometimes even hate the sight of food
Always told to be sexy and bold till his words killed the esteem in my every mood
But I was so blind to it all, I felt his need to be embarrassed of me was not at all rude
And that me being a fat pig unable to reach my goal was even more indecent and lewd
I feel sick when I eat and more every time he said I was BIG but meant I was fat
So I walked everyday and did sit ups or crunches to make my stomach flat
Because I wanted to be that girl he desired and I believed that body was all I lack
His words were my wounds and so I throw up till I am weak laying on my back.

Statistics show that 1 in 5 women suffer from an eating disorder.
70 million individuals are affected by eating disorders worldwide, with 24 million being American.

1 Corinthians 7:19,23 The important thing is obeying GOD's commandments. You all were bought at a great price, so do NOT become slaves of people.

RACIAL REDEMPTION

The KKK in the south today is so very much thriving and alive,
Racism is a pain and as a society a worse pain shall soon arrive.
There are still white hoods holding rallies and crosses still burn…
And the memory of Martin Luther King in our minds does churn.
He made Eve from Adams rib and every color and race is here to give,
He made us different and unique so we can together in harmony live…
Learning from each other and expanding thru diversity to loving over hate.
Finding the holy-grail as Jesus did by kindness of others is our fate.
Another black man killed, another child born interracially mixed,
Hung from a tree on a dirt road like Jesus on a bloody crucifix…
A man dragged by a truck for a few miles as limbs cracks and dismembered.
There was a speech called "I have a Dream" can we all remember?
Hating someone because a color of skin pigment echo's intimidation.
Because you fear anything you don't know about in your need for salvation.
He said that you are all from the dust of the earth, all his very own creation.
But your ignorance to loathe is more common of a sin than fornication.
We shall aspire to desire to make Earth GOD's promised land…
Remembering we were all made from the very palm of his hand….
He made us each special, unique and knows the name of every woman and man.
Our differences were made to come together for the use of his greater plan.
Racial Redemption, the pursuit we need to follow in our steps to greatness,
Educating beyond what society and television has taught in all this fakeness.
Guns are clicking and violence is rampant in our conscious of lateness….
And politicians use gender and race to make comments that are tasteless.
Another hate crime has been committed and you are now on trial….
For the noose on society that made division in this country so vile.
Another dirt road and burning crosses, white hoods, a body choking on bile,
Who made you so eager to take someone's life and make it defiled.
Racial hate groups live in your neighborhood and breed tormented views,
But the more we step up to acknowledge and by redemption we refuse….
We take back the power to ignite the light and unite in the fight….
To step up and make a difference in this world by doing what is right

Over 10,000 hate crimes happen annually and 51.3 percent are motivated by racial bias, most of these crimes are acts of violence….

Galatians 3:8
There is neither Jew nor Greek, slave nor free, male nor female, for you are all one in Christ Jesus.

SPEAK UP

Speak up for me now, I am too damn tired and weak…
I am crying for help, to find the peace that I seek.
Tell me to leave him, please give me the strength to go on.
You know what he is doing , and that it is so very wrong.
He is your friend, so you tell yourself it's not there or real…
I wish for one moment you could experience the pain that I feel.
I want you to step into my abuse, my very private hidden despair,
Maybe if you felt that low, then the cuts would make you care
Speak Up now for I have no voice from yelling and screaming….
This is a real everyday chaos not a bad nightmare you are dreaming.
Speak Up now, aren't you suppose to be my real friend…
My shame has been buried so deep that it makes me live in pretend.
All the signals and signs have been looking you in the face…
Please help me now and don't let me die so disgraced….
Step into my shoes again, now you feel him beat you down.
Lay in your own blood and feel his boot on your head as you lay on the ground.
Feel my fear, the physical illness of covering all these lies…
The days I say I am ok but you hear those very aching in my cries….
Now you can feel what I didn't want you to know or even care to wonder…
When will you speak for me, when my body lays six feet under

If You do not speak up against domestic violence then you accept it in our society ,more woman under the age of 30 die at the hands of their significant other or spouse than by any other cause of death, and 3 million women will be physically abused this year.

A man is to love his wife as he loves his own body; to nurture her and treat her kindly and tenderly
Ephisians 6:21-33

Growing Beast

Every night in the streets another police escapade,
prostitutes, assault, drunks, the average drug-trade.
Our children play where a dead body once laid,
hustlers take no prisoners they just wanna get paid.
Young mothers break the law so their children can eat,
Rosa Parks refused to stand and she took her seat.
Women keep your respect and men please don't beat,
Children repeat what they see in the home and street.
Sweet dreams to the suburbs and those people of power,
where will you be when it is the final hour?
Corruption you make leaves a taste that is sour,
the streets you forget build a hateful tower.
Marches have passed but our nation finds no peace,
injustice happens every day and will not cease.
families participate in unity to the very least,
Loosing our children to streets is a growing beast.

Violence is the number one killer for children ages 15 to 24, over 2.4 million children are diagnosed ADD or ADHD a year and only 1 in 4 children receive medical treatment or help, 30 to 60 violent acts in the home are by people who witnessed domestic violence as children and mental illness and violence are linked in over 80 percent of these cases,

PROVERBS 22:6 Train up a child in the way he should go; even when he is old he will not depart from it.
GENESIS 18:19 For I have chosen him, that he may command his children and his household after him to keep the way of the LORD by doing righteousness and justice, so that the LORD may bring to Abraham what he has promised him."
DEUTERONOMY 6:6-7 These words that I am giving you today are to be in your heart. Repeat them to your children. Talk about them when you sit in your house and when you walk along the road, when you lie down and when you get up"

Jane Doe

Jane Doe was just a crack head who wondered the streets at night,
she was searching for the answers and yearning to live right.
I would preach to her and her smile would become bright,
she said "I love Jesus" and then God took her to the light.
Nobody paid her any attention or tried to show her love,
compassion and grace have met her in the heavens above.
People never stopped to speak and never tried to reach,
who said a crack head is unworthy of what you preach.
Church people sometimes believe they are better than "Jane Doe",
because they don't see the person only the sin of a hoe.
How can we elevate our minds if we don't help people grow,
God's light is for everyone and unconditionally will flow.
Jane Doe saw you preaching and ran the other way,
because you had no kindness in the words you would say.
Condemnation in your voice as you commanded her to pray,
waiving your righteousness and saying in hell she would lay

Approximately 35.9 million Americans aged 12 and older have tried cocaine at least once in their lifetime, An average of 2000 people per day try crack for the first time according to a national survey, and about 2.1 million Americans are regular users. One health danger of crack cocaine use is when cocaine and alcohol are consumed at the same time. When these substances are mixed, the human liver combines cocaine and alcohol and manufactures a third substance, coca ethylene. This intensifies crack cocaine's euphoric effects, while also increasing the risk of sudden death. Most crack cocaine-related deaths are a result of cardiac arrest or seizures followed by respiratory arrest.....An estimated 15,000 people die a year from crack cocaine.

SKIN DEEP

Beauty in America is only skin deep,
we forget honor, love, loyalty and deeper we seep.
We don't jump into judgment we are fast to leap,
because we are immune to hatred and forget to weep.
It is only skin deep when a bullet wounds flesh,
but only the soul will speak when you take your last breath.
Flesh upon flesh and millions of people die from HIV,
walking wounded mentally, we all try to break free.
Women flaunt their naked bodies as a success-full industry,
because people buy sex and they are commitment free.
Women starve themselves to death to be seen as beauty,
killing yourself is not the image you thought we would see.
It was only skin deep when Jesus was nailed to a cross,
but his blood washed away for our sins as the loss.
It was only skin deep as he wore the crown of thorns,
and only in our flesh, for flesh we shall mourn,

Over 10.2 million Surgical and non-surgical COSMETIC procedures are done yearly because people believe they must alter themselves to become beautiful to magazine or society standards.

1 Peter 3:4 But let your adorning be the hidden person of the heart with the imperishable beauty of a gentle and quiet spirit, which in God's sight is very precious.
1 Samuel 16:7 But the Lord said to Samuel, "Do not look on his appearance or on the height of his stature, because I have rejected him. For the Lord sees not as man sees: man looks on the outward appearance, but the Lord looks on the heart."

We Choose To Allow

We, the Society, allow and pretend we do not see things as they are…
We allow the drunk driver to leave the bar and kill with his car.
We allow drug dealers in schools but won't allow religion or prayer.
Courts allow junkies to raise kids but not spanking with care.
We allow racism and violence by turning our heads like it is not there
We allow gangbanging and sexuality exposure pretending were unaware.
We allow every seven minutes another adolescent suicide
We allow politics to overpower morality and we just watch and abide.
We allow husbands to beat their wives and one just died.
We allow television, radio, and magazines to be fact of news,
We allow common people to shape and censor our views.
We allow budget cuts on welfare but can't veto a tax or gun bill…
We allow funding for space travel but hungry children have stomachs to fill.
We allow missing soldiers of captivity, for years to be tortured and kept,
We allow gas price gouging, as aids flourishes, so tears will be wept.
We allow people to go un-medicated, uneducated and unfed….
We allow people to bash gay people and another is found dead.
We allow slavery by condoning prostitution and she is only fourteen…
We allow men to call women bitches when she is meant to be a queen.
We allow our economy to consume, as a rapist walks free on bail…
We allow weapons to enter our country thru the U.S. mail
We allow anorexia because we glamorize, skinny small and frail.
We allow the destruction of America by believing that God will fail.

**PSALM 7:11,12 God judgeth the righteous, and God is angry with the wicked every day.
If he turn not, he will whet his sword; he hath bent his bow, and made it ready.
Proverbs 17:15 He who justifies the wicked and he who condemns the righteous are both
alike an abomination to the Lord.**

DYSFUNCTIONAL FAMILY

Wounds so invisible that even you forgot they were buried that deep
And as you move forward and elevate your awareness, somewhere they repeat.
Dysfunction that arises in verbal abuse, and cruelness that makes you weep.
People that say they love you so much but use your flaws as an excuse to mistreat.
So easy to escape if you never go home to see the past that made you pretend,
That your Daddy, wasn't drinking and that the guy with your mom was just a friend.
That your cousins really weren't smoking crack and Uncles said rules were to bend.
That molestation and addiction were more common than a gambling binge to spend.
American Families have turned into institutions of wrong learning and false direction.
Your American teen does not need the sex talk he learned at 8 all about an erection.
Your drug addicted Aunt lands in jail because her cry for help is to get your attention.
That alcoholic, man whoring niece of yours is using sex to find some affection….
Family dinners have turned into fast food drive ups and single mothers working late.
While the "white supremacist" neighbor teaches your kids a new kind of hate…
There are no more excuses you give to yourself to make yourself believe all is great,
Because, at this very moment a sex offender is online, with your child as the bait….
We believe we can outgrow our family dysfunction, but don't try to mend and heal.
We say we will do things differently but now kids shoot up the school during a lunch meal.
Because instead of learning and correcting a new generation we try to be " keeping it real"
As we numb our own pain of crucified emotions a whole generation is for the devil to steal.
I don't know any perfect family but emotional bonds have been broken and bleed.
We can try to escape into an abyss of delusion or face the fact that parents smoke weed.
Children are growing up watching you pour those gin and tonics after work as you need.
And your denial of your own downfalls plants in that child another, very negative seed….
You may not be abusive and you may be overcompensating for the losses of stability…
But no matter if you're the enabler or the wounded heart with great sensitivity….
The moment you don't be still and stand in belief for the promise of GOD's creativity
You have then lost the battle against the dysfunctional family with great agility

Over 18.5 million Home visits are done a year by social service departments in America to families experiencing clinical dysfunction

1 TIMOTHY 5:8 "Now if anyone does not provide for his own relatives, and especially for his household, he has denied the faith and is worse than an unbeliever"

GODS FURY

When Heaven creates roaring thunder and winds begin to gust..
Do you think God is looking down in disappointment at our lust.
Lust for worldly possessions as we fight against the rush…
We are always, wanting more, unsatisfied by Gods' gifts so plush.
Destruction comes fast to all those who did not hush….

Hush…quietly and heed to God, for we have shown mistrust…
So we provoke the fury that through tornado winds will thrust.
God is showing us his fury and he is revealing his disgust.
He is showing us a glimpse of his wrath because revelation is a must.

Through uncontrollable weather, God shows us how he controls the scene.
Showing us our envy was green, attitude bad and presence mean,
Society directed the belief that money and power only gleam.
In a moment of disaster we all call upon God so we can lean…
Yet everyday our agenda is self promotion, and wrong focus to scheme.

People are controlled by ego and their flesh burns like gasoline
We hold our hand to the gate of hell for a dollar and a dream
Our hearts are full of hatred and only God can make them clean,
The spiritual warfare has begun and the Lord is about to be seen.
When God unleashes his fury will you be one of those who scream?
Will you hold the gate of hell or struggle in faith to carry his beam?

<u>Revelation 11:19</u> And the temple of God which is in heaven was opened; and the ark of His covenant appeared in His temple, and there were flashes of lightning and sounds and peals of thunder and an earthquake and a great hailstorm.

This Could Be You

You will become frail, skinny and your bones and muscles very weak,
Friends you have now will back off if they know, and won't be there to seek.
You are now Treated like a criminal but never actually ever committed a crime…
When you need people the most for support and life is running out of time.
No longer can you go out with people and live the life you once had…
Never did you think you would contract a disease they link to being morally bad
And people believe in myths that it is a plague given to those who live like whores
But there you are sunk in cheeks, cracked lips and skin covered by open soars
We forget that HIV kills you and me and more than the Vietnam war…
Reality is that AIDS is killing every gender, class and human kind as a race….
millions of people are dying but you only pay attention if it is a famous face.
Simply exposed by blood transfusions, sex or even back in the day getting high
But that simple moment transformed into knowing that you will ultimately die
And there is no one who is beyond its reach or completely immune
But just ignorant to the statistics that are singing you a very sad tune….
A melody of madness echoing in our society but not really being heard
Because Aids is still spreading like a wild fire and getting its last word…
Its screaming out that this could easily happen and this could be you….
And yet you drink and don't think that being at risk is something to fear as true
And they get pneumonia very easy and lungs fill with water unable to breath,
A common day with a cold is filled with fever ,chills, sweats and dry heaves
And then the pills don't do as much so you inject meds under the long sleeves
And family won't take care of them or even sip out of their dish washed glass
Because FEAR instead of education is a mindset we must overcome to surpass
And yet this could be you because he looked clean and was from upper middle class,
Ignorance makes us believe you must be dirty and it doesn't attack a certain mass
This could be you, even as you walk around looking as if you are so healthy
Because it doesn't only kill poverty stricken people but also the very wealthy
This could be you, because you helped someone bleeding with an open incision
This could be you because of a split second moment you made a bad decision
This could be you because that girl or guy kept a secret habit or addiction
And because getting tested and being safe is precaution and not a prescription.

**JUDE 1:7 Just as Sodom and Gomorrah and the surrounding
cities, which likewise indulged in sexual immorality and pursued unnatural desire, serve
as an example by undergoing a punishment of eternal firc.
AIDS AWARENESS –GET EDUCATED**

JUSTICE

What is justice in a world where adultery is accepted….
Where people decide what people should be lethally injected
Where taxes pay for houses and food for the insanely infected
Where children of two races must fear of being rejected
Where courtrooms let child predators free to again molest
Where women spend thousands to have a bigger better breast….
When tonight the pavement is a bed for a child's head to rest
What is justice when we give other countries medicine and bread,
And children in America are still starving to be fed …..
What is justice for the child cut from Medicaid who just died?
What brings us justice if budget cuts leave children unsupplied
When drug dealing as an income has held a family down for years
When conviction of the crime leaves a family homeless in fear
Where were you social services to wipe that child's tear?
You recycled those people to pacify something you didn't want to hear…
America is filled with overworked parents doing drugs and drinking beer.
What is the justice when supermodels starve themselves for beauty
Icons are false and political figures receive sex while on duty…
What is justice when the bond of marriage has become a tax junction
And disability again denied a man with no legs who barely can function
What is justice when men of power abuse the poor, sleep with a whore
And basically forget about the people who live right next door…..
Are we so blinded by police who take bribes, a media that lies
Or are we just a nation that does not care if it dies?
What is justice if we stay in such bondage but call this the land of the free
What is justice if you only care what happens to you and not me?
What is justice in a world where only money is societies steeple?
When honesty can be bought and so can the faith of most people….
What is justice for a battered wife whose only way was murder
Sentenced to years, with no more fears, that he can ever hurt her?
What is justice for a crack-head, is being a junkie the crime?
We give a drug addict a sentence because rehabilitation wastes our time?
What is justice if our judgment of character is yours and mine?

Proverbs 29:26 Many seek the face of a ruler, but it is from the Lord that a man gets justice.
Mathew 7:1-2"Judge not, that you be not judged. For with the judgment you pronounce you will be judged, and with the measure you use it will be measured to you.

HUMANITY

How holy are we as a Nation? Is there any faith left in people?
How much light do we shine down from an optimistic steeple?
What happened to our morals? What happened to our pride?
Can people really overlook the homeless and buy a pimped out ride?
Are we really that vain? Are we really that self centered and shallow?
Do we really not think of others, have our hearts become that hollow?
We don't stop and help the woman in the street being beaten by her mate,
And people look with disgust at others happy but stop to watch violent hate.
Kids don't open the doors for elderly and men don't open car doors for a date,
When did we learn to disregard the very core of what made us so great?
America was the promise land where you had all opportunity to achieve.
So when did we become a country that no longer seems to even grieve.
You can blame music videos, fashion magazines or deceptive preachers
But that does not take away the fact that you are your child's teachers.
Militia groups are in high schools, the KKK and Farrakhans's words in the "Last Call"
For No Man is beyond saving, or bigger than GOD's hand that catches every fall…
You give them luxury and take away spanking, discipline and prayer in school,
And then you don't teach them work and wonder why these children act so much a fool?
You make time to go to the bar or the local party and drive drunk with your car….
But making time for your kids or church on Sunday would be going way too far?
You can bow to Buddha, pray to saints and meditate and never get the real view,
Religion or good deeds can't take you as far, as the spirit of GOD in you….
Until you find GOD's peace the war on our souls to be righteous will not cease….
And destruction toward our death toll in this nation will grow like a futile beast.
Mentally in this nation we are creating and expanding our own prison,
Because we need to keep changing this world, for the better and holding the vision.
Maybe if we saw each other again as brothers and sisters in GODs family…
Than we can change this world back into a place where there is humanity.

Ephesians 4:32 Be kind to one another, tenderhearted, forgiving one another, as God in Christ forgave you.
Ephesians 4:2 With all humility and gentleness, with patience, bearing with one another in love,

My First Time Speechless

She sat in the clinic in a quiet, sad, distressed catatonic state
She kept asking the front desk nurse "How long is the wait"
Her eyes looked back at me as I stayed behind in the waiting room
I stared at the janitor and back and forth went his broom…
I could not look at the faces of those women in such terror and gloom
Goose bumps rose from my skin as I could see their fear of such doom
And then I could hear her screams as the baby was ripped from the womb
I tried so hard to get to her but they said I could not go in
They said she would be fine just needed some extra sutures very thin
I waited watching wounded souls and four more hours had gone by
Women after women came out and each one had a painful cry
They said she needed to sleep a bit, maybe another whole hour
I heard her crying my name and became that person who had no power
And so when she awoke, pale chalky dry throat her face was a dying flower
And the first thing she said was my baby is dead and I heard the bones devour
She explained all the pain of hearing the bones break and my knees began to tower
Her story so explicit that she felt the death of a soul sucked out of her with suction
I could hardly think after that my mind just numbed so that I could barely function
Too weak to walk, I carried her crying, passing protesters screaming at the car
But she motioned to vomit and said "please don't drive very far"
And before I knew it she was passed out in vomit face down on the ground
She mumbled very few words and painful heart aching disturbing sound
She looked into my face with tears glistening like diamonds off her skin
Then she whispered in a faint weep "I killed my own baby an immortal sin"
She cried "Imagine how you would feel if you had to kill your own child?'
My first time speechless a moment I could not get over in my mind for a while

1,6 million women make this choice, as abortions are performed every year in America, that is a rate of one unborn baby that dies every 20 seconds and women scarred for life…

<u>Jeremiah 1:5</u> Before I formed you in the womb I knew you, before you were born I set you apart; I appointed you as a prophet to the nations.

Mentally Unhealthy Child

I was about 7 or 8 years old when they notice that my issues were affecting my physically
And as a highly dyslexic child called stupid and dumb every day I was numb as habitually
So until all my eyelashes were gone and bald spots were more seen than covered noticeably
They realized not just my learning skills were hurting but something more of sociably

I was that weird kid who would sit for hours and pick my hair strand by strand
As if I would reach euphoria or bliss as the hair had seep between my fingers in hand
Maybe I was just the ugly kid who thought I was so different like a distorted brand..
And mutilation of myself was fine because the popular people won't let me in their land

Emotional freedom when I pulled real hard from my scalp as if it were a blissness
Everyone else controlled me by the names I was called, but I controlled my sickness
Anxiety daily ,anguish to learn and other people always reminding how I was less…
A disease in my mind and a depression out of control yelling mayday from distress

So young and yet my demons ,abuse, battles and guilt lay so heavy in my chest
And it was easier for Adults to say I was crazed than my real issues be seen or addressed
This is something I never thought I would share or write publicly in a forum to confess
But the battle in me was clearly I see just the self worth and hate at the cusp of its crest

My scalp was hairless, eyelashes gone like a fish and bald spots smooth and white
But after seeking help and finding so many others suffer in silence I made this my fight
Because pulling your hair out, cutting with a razor and suicide attempts rise every night
Hopeless despair and depression are real even if you try to keep them out of public sight

Trichotillomania, also known as compulsive hair pulling, is a disfiguring and emotionally painful disorder. It is estimated that the number of hair pullers in the United States alone, include as many as 5% of the US population and 1 in 2 people of every 50 pull their hair at some stage of life. An estimated 2.5 million people exhibit some type of self abuse behavior .

Chapter Two:

Climbing A Bridge To Change

Let The Bridge Burn

Live your day as if it were your last,
Look to your future and forget your past.
Character is the element that makes a great man,
People have a vision, but God has a master plan.
People find ways to live with their own deceit,
A person who does not try will never gain to defeat.
It is not what you did but how you made it correct,
It is how you change the negative to a positive effect.
Be better than the people who hurt and scorned you,
spiritual law brings their actions, back by two.
Prejudice tendencies and bias people took the wrong road,
because energy bounces back to the reaper who sewed.
Spiritual growth will bring you into elevation,
Acceptance by others will bring you expectation.
Do what you yearn as you live just to learn,
Sometimes it is better, just to let the bridge burn

Mark 9:43
And if thy hand offend thee, cut it off: it is better for thee to enter into life maimed, than having two hands to go into hell, into the fire that never shall be quenched:

The Gaps that break your bridge:

Mistakes can either make us or break us but the way we view them and learn gives us opportunity to change or repeat the things that cause us pain..I am not a Christian leader, a Saint or anywhere near being a perfect person and I have made some of the most self destructive decisions and bad choices a person can make hurting many people I love. Amazing Grace found me and the truth is that I am sinner unworthy of the forgiveness and undeserving of the blood that was shed on a cross for all my inequities and repulsive sins in this world. Pain and Anguish kept me from climbing the mountain or even attempting to believe I could try .God had forgiven me but I chose not to forgive myself and so I kept stumbling over the same rocks of deception. The big rock of self hate, the pebble of other people's opinions, the stick in the road called anger and the snakes bites I acquired standing still kept me from climbing .Then I realized all these gaps had the attention and energy of my mind instead of being in focus at where the bridge would lead my heart. What could I possibly think would change and what would be at the end of the bridge after all of my struggling to get there. The very simple answer is GOD's grace ,mercy and love. The bridge is your mending heart, the gaps are the obstacles that build your character, the climb is the test of your faith and the change is what you made in burning bridges or filling the gaps. Redirect your thought form to see what you are seeking and not what you are trying to run from and make the ultimate goal to find the peace in your soul. Somewhere the shaking bridge finds a sturdy foundation when you make the decision that your climb is to find God.

I Chronicles 16:11 Seek the LORD and his strength, seek his face continually.
Psalms 105:4 Seek the LORD, and his strength: seek his face evermore.
Isaiah 55:6 Seek ye the LORD while he may be found, call ye upon him while he is near

Shattered Image

Never did I believed in my beautiful self but only darkness that existed,
I soaked my childhood pains in alcohol, both hands held tight to bottles I double fisted…..
At the bar I could blend so well as the funny girl that made you laugh while you got twisted,
Conquer and drink as I didn't think but took a man home to make myself feel
lifted…

Shattered Self Image, I give you my inadequate actions, flaws ,issues and evil sin,
Because exposing myself raw leaves no room for the devil to stand up and grin

Because it was easy to justify ,live a lie and deny than live up to what GOD had gifted.
Rough times in my mind where my soul was empty and being adorable made me so elated,
The attention from different men, never knew then, would be something I used and hated.
Needing to be what you saw as beauty because inside my own worth was cut and jaded
But blind to see, the better in me, I chose to agree because my mind was always faded….
And life had become so comfortably numb because so many people liked me medicated

Shattered Self Image, I give you my inadequate actions, flaws ,issues and evil sin,
Because exposing myself raw leaves no room for the devil to stand up and grin

Wild as a child, a little hostile had a talent and a dream that made me ignorant and vile
Because people would expect greatness and vision but my own uniqueness I did defile….
Ran with the in crowd, was boisterous and loud but the party girl was just my style,
And why would I go against the grain to find the pain I hadn't owned up to for a while…
Because the narrow sober road I sought to live would only take me out of my own denial.

Shattered Self Image, I give you my inadequate actions, flaws ,issues and evil sin,
Because exposing myself raw leaves no room for the devil to stand up and grin

Self Sabotage, Destruction of Self Esteem, that I would never find until sober and clean
Bitterness stole my heart and I gave drugs more power to take away my own dream
Because I only knew how to like myself when I was Angry at everything in between…
And I couldn't see beyond my walls to find a place in GOD where I could lean….
and misery loves equal company so people feared how brightly that I could gleam

Shattered Self Image, I give you my inadequate actions, flaws ,issues and evil sin,
Because exposing myself raw leaves no room for the devil to stand up and grin

I made my bed, sold my soul and tried to stay blind to my own Damascus Road,
Because ignorant to heal was easier than trying to carry the responsible load
And hurting from the pain was more unbearable than being heartless and cold
And standing up in conviction takes more strength than to quit and to fold....
So we hide in our own weakness because we fear our own strength in being bold.

Shattered Self Image, I give you my inadequate actions, flaws ,issues and evil sin,
Because exposing myself raw leaves no room for the devil to stand up and grin

Afraid to let go of people we love, because we do not want them to go away
We stay stagnant and delay as if no actions from us will make GOD sway
But we can't barter or negotiate a blessing if we are holding tight to the decay
exposing yourself to come what may is how you stand firm in the truth you say
So cut yourself to get the correct way and bleed to save a soul as a price you pay

John 10:10 The thief comes only to steal and kill and destroy. I came that they may have life and have it abundantly.

CHASE GOD...........

The preacher was almost done with his sermon when something stopped him in his track,
He said GOD wants to speak to the girl with the poems who hides her face way in the back.
He pointed me out and told me to stand up and rise to the podium from the back pew....
He said GOD wants to bestow great blessings that he has been sending to you.

Then he told me to pause my walk to the alter and yelled for me to extend out my hands.
He said your talent radiates off you like fire and fiercely you will use it to touch every land.
He told me to take a few more steps forward and he paused as his body started to shake.
I see your past of darkness, torment, torture, excruciating pain that makes you want to break.

Then he bent in a sickening motion as he jerked and gasped out an overwhelming cry...
His eyes showed horror as he asked me how many times can the devil try to make you die?
All the people in the church stared at me but the words of the preacher would not retreat.
He said you have so much power in the gift GOD gave you that it breathes from your head to
feet.

Why do you think GOD wakes you from a sound sleep with words in the middle of the night?
Why do you think other people's pain is felt in your soul and you pray for them with fight?
You are a warrior anointed by his touch, make them CHASE GOD or they die not knowing
his light.
How many times does GOD have to tell you to be his vessel, flowing in every word that you
write....

He said GOD had a reason to save you from that man that beat every part of you so violent,
He did not reach down and rip you from the pits of hell so that you could stay this silent.
He did not allow you to experience rape, addiction, poverty, loss, abuse and pain with no
reason.
Because you must use it to write the words that make them CHASE GOD and this is the
season!

Prodigal, you spoke in tongues by the age of seven and have been baptized more than a few....
You can break satans back with the words that you write like GOD has commanded you to do,
Why do you choose not to believe your worthy and hide your face in the churches back pew?
People need someone to tell them to CHASE GOD in a gripping way and that's why he chose
you.

The preacher leaned close to my face as his hand covered in oil reached toward my forehead,
He said CHASE GOD and in a blink of an eye I saw the crucifix and souls crying from the dead.
When the anointed oil touched my skin I could see the blood of Jesus pouring out so red.....
I heard a thundering voice say tell them to CHASE GOD that is why I sent my son and he bled.

When I opened my eyes, laying on the floor of the church my lungs felt like they drowned.
But the words CHASE GOD were echoing in my ears and I could hear no other human sound......
CHASE GOD until your weary CHASE GOD till exhausted, CHASE GOD everyday until he is found.
Tell them CHASE GOD so that people are saved before the devil destroys and takes them down.

The preacher smiled at me as I arose from the floor and said GOD has told you what to speak
CHASE GOD is the message he wants you to write for the Christians only pretending to be meek.
CHASE GOD is the most powerful lesson for you to teach the sinning souls too fragile and weak.
CHASE GOD is the words you shall deliver for even believers who cannot find what they seek....
CHASE GOD for yourself because he thinks you are someone special he has been waiting to meet.

Power Of Words

A word can be a blessing as you speak it or it can become a person's curse,
Every word we verbalize does energize and ripples effect into our Universe.

The power of intention in what we say will always create that which we will do,
The power of your words are hate and love and effect many people as well as you.

Let no corrupt word against another be deceitful or injure them in deceit to fail
Yet be the inspiration and uplifting power that can give them power to set sail

If you answer to what people call you in this life eventually you may become it,
Because we acquire a knowledge in our mind when people tell us to give up or quit

And we make excuses because we may believe in those words and then they will fit,
As many books in the Bible have testified to sanctify the words that lead you to the pit

Warnings surround you when you say something bad then you later feel real sad,
And then you may apologize or correct those lies and the energy lifts you to glad.

Words are like knives crippling other people in their mind and spirit with pain,
Or promise of Abundance because you spoke to claim it and then it was there to gain.

Have you ever told someone you loved them to keep them but knew you really didn't
And then suddenly when they left your side how powerful love engulfed you in it...

The power of life and death are in the tongue so be careful of your unkind speech
The more attention you give to something makes it grow so negative must cease
Because the energy of peace and harmony is the vibration you want to release....

Have you called someone names such as unattractive, stupid, crazy or even fat?
When they acted crazier, or ugly inside and grow bigger did you see how you did that?

Have you berated someone or belittled a person and then someone then did it to you,
Because what you give in energy and create with words strengthens power back in two.

So keep no wickedness in thought or allow destruction to seep from your lips to decay
Because life and death are in your tongue and there is great power in everything you say.

Bible references to the power of words: Ephisians 4:29,Proverbs 21:23, 1 Peter 3:10
Psalm 141:3, James 1:26, Proverbs 10:9, 15:23, 1 Corinthians 14:19,Isaiah
50:40,Eccliesiastes 10:12-14
Psalms 55:21 His speech is smooth as butter, yet war is in his heart; his words are more soothing than oil, yet they are drawn swords.

God has simply chosen us and he wants to love us in our times of need and struggle. Acceptance of our mission to make this world a better place can define our role in this world as a positive one. His mercy is upon us daily and his love is unmeasured and limitless. We will be held accountable for our speech, actions and decisions in this lifetime but there will never be anything that can separate us from god's love. Today know that you matter to god and reflecting his love and light can create a life you always dreamed of. It is never what has happened to us on our journey but how we changed and educated others with our knowledge. Anger is a human emotion and can be used properly as a motivation and not a vengeance. The actions of others never define us and our interpretation of circumstances is the crossroad of our mind that we can use in any way. Today remember people will always fail you, but god never will . loving in an unconditional way should always have the knowledge that people will harm you inevitably, but you prepare to remain in love and harmony when it does. The choice of proving yourself correct or engaging in any conflict opposes GOD in every way. So remember that the end result of forgiveness and being kind to those who hurt us is more powerful than any other element of GOD's Laws. The ten commandments have 4 laws respecting GOD and 6 laws respecting others. The fruits of the spirit are felt by people we encounter and can change any atmosphere to elevate us as we love each other the way it is written to do so. Choose change, create life and follow the path that leads into the promise land of abundance. Forgiveness starts with yourself and becomes the ability to love in the most awful circumstance of difficulty which becomes your greatest strength and attribute in this lifetime.

BITTER OR BETTER

There are days when I wish to let go of my bible and be bitter instead of better
I feel like I make no difference so why not be like those chasing the money as a go getter
Days I feel like I live up to nobody expectations of me and want to write a dear John letter
Then those who once taunted my decline now need my helping hand and not my vendetta.
It has all been done before and you are so not different than me in your reprise…
They took one look up and down, than eye to eye and in a moment saw your size.
But people's interpretation, and sizing you up in just a moment takes them by surprise,
Because they never expect the person they destroyed to be the person hearing their cries.
People never expect a hand from a face that they have slapped real hard into a wall.
Being a vessel of GOD means you jump to the task even when it is a hard call…
You must swallow your pride, digest the anger and decide if you are Paul or Saul?
Are you going to be less of a person because you can injure them now or go tall?
It takes a strong soul to care for the unkind, to be a prayer warrior and walk the line,
You don't really want to help this uncaring, manipulative, abusive piece of slime…
But if you are bitter and not better than you become just as corrupt & rotten as the swine,
And you lost touch with the very great forgiveness that helps you be exceptionally divine.
Bitter or better, a choice that holds the power to make or break your soul…
The task, that is given to so many people daily and stealing what makes them whole.
The very sin that keeps them from heaven and on a wrong path where peace is stole.
The very choice that can allow you to fly with Angels or bury you in very hot coal….
My redemption is in my action and it must be pure in my heart, where it bled.
Bitterness can prevent any action from being great and tear it all to shred….
You are everything you do and have power in every word that is spoken and said.
Bitter or better is more than a choice because it is a way to speak life to things dead.
Dormant anguish arises like that dream of getting even or that opportunity of spite.
But that same dead dog lying needs bandages even when his sharp teeth do bite.
Trust me there is no dilemma in your soul to choose what is wrong and what is right.
But there is a choice of being better than bitter just like choosing darkness over the light.

Romans 12:19 Beloved, never avenge yourselves, but leave it to the wrath of God, for it is written, "Vengeance is mine, I will repay, says the Lord."
Hebrews 12:15 Look after each other so that not one of you will fail to find God's best blessings. What out that no bitterness takes root among you, for as it springs up it causes deep trouble, hurting many in their spiritual lives.

Fairytale Awoken

If you think you can't be yourself as elegant, educated and outspoken ....
Then the world taught you to be a women who remains so sadly broken
Because GOD's said your valued like gold but society treats you like a token
And women are still being mislead and devalued by a fairytale to be awoken

Bedtime Stories end with Prince Charming, sweeping a girl off her feet
Taught that the glory were told by the story that pretty girls never weep
And misguided fairytales that end with sails that every trail will be so sweet
And that if we act correct then maybe we'll get a good man as our final treat

If you are that pretty girl who only needs a good man to get her ahead in life,
The woman that thinks the highest goal is to be known as just a rich man's wife.
Then you are just societies slave to be engaged in a false hope of all that hype
That women are defined by others as less or inadequate, if your just not his type.

Sex in the city, oh how Barbie doll pretty, we all try to be a character of mirage
But if you downplay ,get told by the snippy PTA, what you should do or say....
You Fear being different, bold or tough, cause they may say you are gay
Then you are keeping the true unique beauty from within you hidden at bay

If you think you can't be yourself as elegant, educated and outspoken ....
Then the world taught you to be a women who remains so sadly broken
Because GOD's said your valued like gold but society treats you like a token
And women are still being mislead and devalued by a fairytale to be awoken...

Funny how a man can buy the cow, but then gets milk somewhere else for free
And then again the false pretend tells us something must be very wrong with me
Fix it we hope yet feel like a joke and the fairytale tells you what to see....
But if you stay and allow that shallow feeling somehow makes us all stay and agree

Just like Leave it to beaver, the perfect man pleaser as a women's role is a deceiver....
They told you if you didn't tolerate his violence or discretions you'll be a griever
Because with no education or money your options end with roads saying neither
So you smile at the table after he degraded your ethics as a Christian believer

Women Can aspire to any greatness but believe in the fairytale of the white night
And when we get college educated instead of berated we get goals in our view of sight
Women with PHD's getting hated by these other women who talk trash with a gripe
Because competition they see when they are guilty of not trying to be more and get right.
Your fairytale is now awoken, get brave and dare to be yourself outspoken and unique
Know yourself and don't bow down because of a man you allowed in your bed to sleep
Skydive, be alive adventure forward boldly outside the box that you allowed to get so steep
Because the fairytale only keeps you waiting on a life that is a step away from your feet,
And a real man can withstand a woman who doesn't defines feminine as mousy, needy or weak.

Colossians 3:19 **Many a man claims to have unfailing love, but a faithful man who can find?**

I CRY.....

I cry for those who cannot change or awake,
for the people who go through life being settled in fake
I cry for the scorned, underdog and mighty triumphant,
God is the only way to live your life more abundant.

I cry for those who cannot or don't want to find their will,
because the empty space they patch but cannot fill
I cry on the dark Road where you can't see the light
I cry that we lack love and learn only hatred to fight

I cry for those who don't know they are educated blind,
the people who look past or ignore what is there to find
Every day we can choose to become a kinder human being,
by opening up your eyes and simply truthfully seeing.

I cry for those who cannot find the road to salvation,
for God's hands are wide open and the only invitation
Yet we are misinformed by leaders that are only imitation
Instead of uplifting we kill each other, every day in this nation

Isaiah 41:10 Fear not, for I am with you; be not dismayed, for I am your God; I will strengthen you, I will help you, I will uphold you with my righteous right hand.
Ezekiel 34:16 I will search for the lost and bring back the strays. I will bind up the injured and strengthen the weak, but the sleek and the strong I will destroy. I will shepherd the flock with justice
1 Corinthians 1:25 For the foolishness of God is wiser than man's wisdom, and the weakness of God is stronger than man's strength.
Psalm 40:1-2 I waited patiently for the Lord; he turned to me and heard my cry. He lifted me out of the slimy pit, out of the mud and mire; he set my feet on a rock and gave me a firm place to stand.

MONEYS LUST

Every American Currency reads to say: "In GOD We Trust"
And yet people kill each other for the belief of moneys lust
And at the end of your life you will enter the ground like dust
And you will not need the things that you believed were a must

People deceive their families, bosses and even a favorite honey
Because somewhere they were taught happiness is linked to money

Embezzlement, laundering or a false quick check card scam
Gave you all the things that bling but never made the man

People are always taking a short cut to making money a quicker way
To be above people or a better class because we respect what the rich say

Believing status is achievement and the only way to be treated like a King
Sadly toys and cars or houses are not character but an empty human thing

Every American Currency reads to say: "In GOD We Trust"
And yet people kill each other for the belief of moneys lust
And at the end of your life you will enter the ground like dust
And you will not need the things that you believed were a must

We compete for validation and success believing it is pure culture
And feed a need for falseness of greed that takes our soul like a vulture

Egos are built by our bank accounts and families not on biblical foundation
Because somewhere American wealth became the forum of our Holy Nation

You can buy diamonds, vacations, technology and fancy clothes cover the shame,
But you're just a lost soul in torment believing peace is found at the top of the game.

We forget moral conduct ,ethics , humanity, and kindness all for monetary gain,
Creating a mirage that we will still go to heaven because power makes you all so vain

Every American Currency reads to say: "In GOD We Trust"
And yet people kill each other for the belief of moneys lust
And at the end of your life you will enter the ground like dust
And you will not need the things that you believed were a must

Attitude

Another angry person creates negative atmosphere,
Take nothing for granted and Thank GOD you are here.
Wake up and look for the laughter and not the tear,
because we bring on situations with laughter and fear.
Your attitude can change the face of a day,
Your reaction to the bad things can make a way.
Remember you create with the words that you say,
and don't forget to stop and kneel down to pray.
We don't smell the roses because we are afraid of thorns,
but another life wished they did as family mourns.
We don't cherish life or people but grab envy's horn,
Instead of uplifting each other we choose to scorn.
We walk away from conflict and strait into self-doubt,
then reach for the sword and chew someone else out.
We are so calculated to anger and we scream and shout,
Who are we to think that we have to run our mouth.
So someone did you wrong, why can't you make a mends,
We live so fake already because we try to alter pretend.
If you are not honest to yourself, it's not your hand to lend,
Spiritual law is negative or positive and doesn't bend.
Don't cut-throat other people in words you speak,
No matter how evil, forgiveness is not that bleak.
If you must feel like a doormat to prove you are meek,
Attitude will bring you the peaceful world that you seek.
Listen and learn and be slow to move those lips,
the one that run's fast is the one who slips.
Listen and learn so you know the snag that trips,
but remember that advice is not always a good tip.
Other people have no answers they are just as confused,
You can question with no answers and stay so amused.
The struggle is our attitude and to change how we choose,
We must understand each other and have compassion of views.

OUR ATTITUDE SCRIPTURES:

Romans 12:19, Luke 18:7... **To Unfairness** — Our attitude should be patience, humility, confident in God's justice.

Psalms 62:5, Jeremiah 17:5, Deuteronomy 32:4, Job 13:15, Romans. 8:28 .... **To Disappointment or Tragedy** — Our attitude should be humility, submission to God, prayerful, confidence in God's fairness.

2 Corinthians 5:18, 2 Peter 3:9, Matthew 18:11-14 ... **To the Lost** — Our attitude should be compassionate, forgiving, encouraging, helpful, reconciling them to God.

Matthew.18:8-9, Galatians 6:1,,...,**To Sin** — Our attitude should be uncompromising, un-accepting, intolerant, unsympathetic, yet compassionate and reconciliatory for the repentant.

Proverbs. 16:18 Jas. 4:6 ..... **To Success** — Our attitude should be humble, grateful, God-glorifying, not self-exalting or forgetful to God.

Colossians 3:13, Mathew. 5:9, Phil 2:14 ....**To Misunderstanding** — Our attitude should be peacemaking, reconciliatory, patient, forgiving.

Ephesians 4:22-23 ..,,. you were taught ... to be made new in the attitude of your minds

Philippians 2:5......Your attitude should be the same as that of Christ Jesus.

Let your mind see the prosperity in the poverty and the smile in the tears for GOD has promised he has your best interest at heart. Let your heart not be in denial of the pain so that it may appreciate the outpour of amazing comfort, Allow yourself to see your flaws for the edification of necessary correction and move forward in learning and accepting so that all may be constructive criticism. See the possibility in rejection and find a conquering spirit for your fear but it all depends on the mindset you choose and the attitude you radiate. Profess and Speak inspiration to every dreadful, darkened thought and you may transform the negative situations into your greatest triumphs. Today choose to have the attitude to BELIEVE.......

If It Wasn't For.......

If it wasn't for those people in my life who always kicked me down,
I would have never learned to fight my way back up or get off the ground.
If it wasn't for my struggle as a single mother learning to wear all the hats,
I wouldn't be able to scrub floors and then wear a suit and read budget stats.

If it wasn't for the cheating ex, or evil corporate ladder and a selfish population.
I would never have traveled outside my realm to see diversity of this nation.
If it wasn't for that homeless man's conversations I might be concerned about greed
And I would have never learned that there are so many hungry Americans we need to feed.

If it wasn't for that boss that taught me that pity is not attractive so loose it....
I would not be boss that I am, learning to have compassion and correctly use it.
If it was not for my own belief in GOD I would never have made it past manipulation
And learned to stand strong with people who try to conquer me with intimidation...

If it wasn't for my faith that has seen me thru the lowest places in the valley of sin,
I would not know how to appreciate the blessings or cherish the struggle to win....
If it wasn't for my failures and rock-bottoms then I would never have learned to endure,
And I would still be waiting on life or fate to drop something amazing at my front door....

If it wasn't for heartache, loves lost, death or destruction that made my heart so soar,
Then I would never have learned my strength is bigger and I can take so much more....
If it wasn't for losing everything in my life and being stripped of all my wealth...
I would never have learned that loneliness makes you truly know yourself...

If it wasn't for random acts of kindness from strangers I would not know charity,
Or how to see which people are real in my life with spiritual clarity....
If it wasn't for all the hardships I experienced in my life I would not have gained strength
Or learned that the love of GOD surrounds me and his grace stretches beyond length.

If it wasn't for all those days of deep depression, pain and struggle that made me want to die
Than I would never have learned to try harder, climb stronger and learned to really fly.

Flightless Bird

I see you are hurt, my flightless bird and I wonder if you have a broken wing…
I reach out to mend you but GOD said to leave you there and to not do a thing…
As I struggle with his will and my own desire to make the caged bird sing…
He tells me that the flightless bird needs to know pain for the blessings he brings…

Flightless does not mean finished and broken does not mean defeated or conquered
If you could see yourself the way I see you then maybe it would echo love responded

Flightless bird, God sent you a lesson to show you again how you can fly….
And what I need to be for you is the inspiration that gives you the will to try…
Flightless bird I won't be the person to hold your wings but I'll let you soar high
And I will remind you of the greatness within you how others envy you and sigh.

Flightless does not mean finished and broken does not mean defeated or conquered
If you could see yourself the way I see you then maybe it would echo love responded

Flightless bird, to fly higher, you need to know the gift of your wings appreciated,
And that for every broken wing I will replace with a greatness when it has faded…
Trust me that you will fly more careful once you have been so very jaded….
Because my will in your life and faith in your heart has never been separated…..

Flightless does not mean finished and broken does not mean defeated or conquered
If you could see yourself the way I see you then maybe it would echo love responded

I see you flightless bird, and I hear GOD begging you to surrender…
Because only he can comfort and change the wounds that seem so tender,
He heals and reconstructs as he protects with angels as your defender…
And when you find his love, my flightless bird will find joy and splendor…
..
Flightless does not mean finished and broken does not mean defeated or conquered
If you could see yourself the way I see you then maybe it would echo love responded

Flightless bird let me see you reach the mountain peek….
Stronger from your struggle flightless did not make you weak……..

Generational Curse

She is what you call a "Dry Alcoholic" who never in her life took a drink
But being raised in the disease so deep that it affected every way you think
Never taught emotionally healthy habits so the patterns repeat like a link
That becomes a curse every generation worse but never in her reality will it sink

Her father was a man who everyone feared and respected in reverence
And at about age 11, he destroyed every feeling I had toward any acceptance
So I was told that when I stood up for myself to him, I should make repentance
And the sick cycle I didn't break but was told to tolerate with no reluctance

I remember why I stayed with a man who broke my teeth with his fist
Because I never wanted to go back home and recognize I had to live with this
That I was always to blame, a whipping post they could abuse and persist
But then she will tell you she's my biggest fan and GOD the story I did twist.

The truth is that at my earliest cry for help, I was 15 and attempted suicide
And the agony and pain of my Grandfather's verbal abuse was what they hide
Even in a counsel office, she would tell them she was leaving because I lied
And not to believe me no matter what I said in session or how hard I cried

No matter what a Medical Professional could agree, or see they just let it be
And still afraid of her own father, because you don't shake any family tree
She then became just like him in a bitter state of hate that never let her free
And I became the rotten apple, because therapy was harder than blaming me

Years of Counseling and searching and thirty years later the cycle does repeat
And I remember not to take it personal because then I allow it power to defeat
And I still know whatever road I take the "dry alcoholic" in her has self deceit
And by allowing myself to take her insults and blame just allows the devil a seat

She claims to be a woman of GOD but on Sunday never even enters a church
And she will tell you she loves me but when were alone her tongue does lurch
Leaping out the same words of her father like a venom to wound on a search
And the "Dry Alcoholic" manipulates to get an upper hand like a bird on a perch

The generational curse we never speak of or deny, to look wholesome and clean
So others never tarnish an image and the real family dynamic never be seen...
The detrimental factor that created hatred between sisters and envy so green
Like a monster in a closet attacking me till I have no family left in love to lean.

The memory that she always looked for his acceptance over her own child
And then I became the adult trying to make her love me, just once in a while
No matter what I do or become in this life , I will always be crucially defiled
Because the generational curse and behavior patterns get worse and not mild.

The Girl He Would Regret

One morning he will awake and reality will set in because I am no longer there….
He will feel the weight of his decisions and excuses that now make his heart care.
All the times he said he didn't need anyone or denied the love he said he could not spare,
Will be the pain that doubles back on him for the days l loved him more than I could bear.

I was his confidant, secret keeper, drinking buddy, cool chick that he only called a friend….
I was the girl who could calm him or argue his sarcasm and damn I could hold down my end,
I was his unconditional love, lady who reminded him of God above, funny text to send….
I was the girl he said he loved to have around but got tired of playing for his pretend.
Because continuing to love him that way gave him freedom and made me only bend.

He will remember how he smiled at the stupid quirky crazy stuff that I said and did….
My sad frown, the echo of my laughter, my soft touch and playful moments acting like a kid.
He will remember the support I gave, respect I earned and code of honor that I live….
The woman who gave more of herself to him while the pain of her tears were very hid.

He said how he really loved me but not in that way, so I let him fly to have wings…..
Because he is not the guy who gets tied down but, why would he when I gave him those things
I was everything the girlfriend is and gave much more than a marriage relationship brings…..
Guess he never thought that what comes around goes around and the pendulum finally swings.

He never saw it coming while complaining about my wining double talk or buzzed sidestep,
He never saw his own love because he was living in a dream about some girl he didn't get……
So my honesty, emotion, love and admiration he overlooked as something he just won't let
Because he was so busy pushing me away he never thought I would be the girl he would regret.

Psalms 147:3 He heals the brokenhearted and binds up their wounds.
Psalms 34:18 The LORD is near to those who have a broken heart, and saves such as have a contrite spirit.

HELTER SKELTER

I fought my way hard to come out of hell-demons pushed me to the edge where I fell.

Roots had my mind and I was under a spell-men were my weakness and the lies they tell.

I brought death to other souls thru the drugs I did sell- I thirsted living water-chose the wrong well.

When flesh was burning-GOD didn't ring the bell- because the purpose of my pain was the story I tell.

HELTER SKELTER-You didn't know how I had felt ya-how many souls lay on your chest

Bear the cross on your back and find your shelter-before you get to the eternal rest

How many souls will lay on your chest when you are casted down to your eternal rest…

The armor of righteousness is my bulletproof vest-I can hear you screaming-smell burning flesh…

That is for all the days you gave satan your best- I feel your pain-see that you are so hexed…

Be vexed for what is next- your saving grace to bondage is the words in the BIBLE'S text..

The Black cloak-the horns ripped at my back-my arms torn up like a heroin track…

I thought I had it all when my pockets were fat-chasing the package not salvation-how slack..,

The evil spirits will come to attack because of all the days that you worshipped the crack.

Never knew GOD was the spirit I lacked until I entered hell and my world went black…

I ignite you a light-like a spark in the dark-principalities of evil can't bite me but still bark,

You see, hell is not full and evil is waiting for you to slip, as it is silently lurking.…

The devil comes to devour and is working but a nail in a palm bled for your hurting…

So don't turn your back –when God lights a path-believe me when I say I lived that wrath.

HELTER SKELTER-You didn't know how I had felt ya- how many souls lay on your chest

Bear the cross on your back and find your shelter- before you get to the eternal rest

I pray for your soul-I get on my knees- hell is not a place I wish on my enemies,

There is only the smell of death-no water, no air, no sun or even trees.…

Only men eating their own flesh and the flesh does bleed- so take head…

This is where your choices lead, so I plant a seed and hope you find GOD in your need

I John 3:8 For this purpose the Son of God was manifested, that He might destroy the works of the devil.

Luke 10:19 I give you the authority to trample on serpents and scorpions, and over all the power of the enemy, and nothing shall by any means hurt you.

ROMANS 10:9-10, 13 That if thou shalt confess with thy mouth the Lord Jesus, and shalt believe in thine heart that God hath raised him from the dead, thou shalt be saved. For with the heart man believeth unto righteousness; and with the mouth confession is made unto salvation. For whosoever shall call upon the name of the Lord shall be saved

Whispers Of A Butterfly Warrior

I am My Fathers Daughter

Sometimes I just miss him, wish we could just have a cup of coffee together,
Talk about the politics on television or argue about moral views or just the weather.

Sometimes I wish he was sitting at the table yelling or just there to be my best friend,
Sometimes I wish the last time that I saw him he was not dead and I could pretend…

That my whole life did not shatter into pieces when he passed and that life did not change
That people he loved become more closer as a family instead of more estranged….

That I became everything he believed I could be and more but instead I chose badly,
That I learned to love more from his loss but instead built bigger walls sadly…

If I could just hear his voice again, when nothing seems to be going right….
If he was just there to tell me that I was just like him and pick myself up and fight.

Instead I hear silence from his death and look at his urn of ashes that sit on my desk,
And remember every lesson he taught me and hold them close to my chest.

Sometimes I just wish that GOD would give him back and nothing had to change…
That I did not have to stand on my, own and learn strength at a different caliber of range.

His life was full, his love of his family was at times distant and magnificent…
I am his legacy in more ways than one and choose to be critically significant…

He lives thru who he taught me to be, even when I choose to be different and unique,
And even when I fail, I am my fathers' daughter in every pursuit of life that I seek.

He is not just a memory but an icon to the mountain that holds my dreams…
The person that always told me that I could be anything and that it is not as hard as it seems.

The person who accepted my faults and fury, my weakness as well as my hard heart,
That taught me to be the person who see's to the end everything that they start.

I am my fathers daughter and have all his traits of anger and kindness that makes me ,
I am the person he believed in even when the rest of the world cannot see…

Sometimes I just miss him, wish we could have a cup of coffee together,
Talk about the politics on television or argue about moral views or just the weather

Running On Empty

God, can you see my exhausted state, can you see me tossing and turning.
Can you see the expression on their faces as their flesh is burning…..
Can you see me coping with those defiant sinners that are finally learning….
Can you see your works are tugging that drug dealer and his mind is now churning.

Did you see that women crying , why do you keep sending them my way?
My strength to be the warrior is thinning as I am on my knees to pray.
Did you think I was bulletproof or did you just know I have the words to say,
Why do I have to go into the crack house for the soul that went astray?

Running On Empty, running at the speed of light…
Running On Empty but determined to make my life right.
Running On Empty, doing God's work late into the night.
Running On Empty and needing GOD to be in my sight.

Did you hear the foul words that bent me like daggers in the heart,
You keep sending me the tarnished ones that like being ripped apart.
Why send me into the darkness to do this work- it doesn't seem smart.
Am I really the only one that must journey to hell and leave my mark?

I am a prodigal, and that means that the devil will chase me down with a knife,
If I didn't bleed, when I hit my knees then GOD could not give me this life.
I must be as faithful to God as a husband is as he stands by his wife….
I must endure spiritual warfare against the beast that comes with such strife.

Running On Empty, running at the speed of light….
Running On Empty but determined to make my life right.
Running On Empty, doing God's work late into the night
Running On Empty and needing GOD to be in my sight.

I am a soul saver, preaching his words where most could not endure.
And I will keep going when my heart is broken and my flesh is tore.
I will speak to those prisoner's, murderers and give God's word to a whore
I will keep walking the journey he gave me even when my feet are soar.

I have a purpose, a mission from God and I cannot detour from this road
No matter how much It rips me, there is warmth to this ice and cold…
You cannot bargain for a soul and my life and yours cannot be sold….
I am a soul saver, who fights for the lost ….and their stories must be told
Running On Empty, running at the speed of light….

Running On Empty but determined to make my life right.
Running On Empty, doing God's work late into the night
Running On Empty and needing GOD to be in my sight

<u>Galatians 6:9</u> And let us not he weary in well doing: for in due season we shall reap, if we faint not.
<u>1 Thessalonians 5:9-10</u> For God has not destined us for wrath, but to obtain salvation through our Lord Jesus Christ, who died for us so that whether we are awake or asleep we might live with him.

Like Simone of Cyrene

Despair enveloped with that foaming feeling in her mouth….
that cold sweat embracing her stomach slowly turning south
She could not fight that need or want, an overtaking urge
Her body could not cope, resist the dope or purge…
Alone, slowly strapping her arm as she shakes and ticks
Lightning in her hallucination she sees the crucifix….
Images will blind what she doesn't want to find….
But God said to her, child you are mine and it is time
And suddenly all her life went from forward to rewind
The needle scraped inside her flesh, ripped inside her vein..
She jabbed it harder and harder till she could feel no pain
And then her body fell hard like she was hit by a moving train
And the water evaporated from her skin just like the rain…
An everyday addict who functioned among you, is that insane
Or was it that you saw her as nothing but just plain
Because helping her gave you nothing in return to gain
Was it her euphoria or your ignorance that's hard to explain
She died on that table on a lonely cold slab of steel
Among doctors and nurses who are trained to heal
As they called the time of death her eyes flickered grey and teal
Her heartbeat bounced back in a moment that seemed so surreal
As scientist those doctors become trained to just not feel
The presence of God came upon them in a way that was so real
The blood of Jesus covered the surgical room floor
A warm wind blew in but no one opened the door…
The crown of thorns appeared on her flesh that tore
Then the cross began to rise up thru her chest once more
He said to them " I shall show you the pain that I had bore "
Because I would have gone to the cross for just one lonely whore
They saw Christ all bloody carrying that 110 pound beam….
He said will you carry my cross like Simone of Cyrene?
Would you do it for her or him, like you do it for me?
Would you let them pierce your palms for one to be free
Would you give yourself completely give your soul to me?
Would you give up your life to follow my lead?
For the sins that I washed in the blood I bleed……
How many bodies will fall before your soul will heed?

<u>LUKE 15:7</u> Just so, I tell you, there will be more joy in heaven over one sinner who repents than over ninety-nine righteous persons who need no repentance.

<u>Titus 2:11-14</u> For the grace of God has appeared, bringing salvation for all people, training us to renounce ungodliness and worldly passions, and to live self-controlled, upright, and godly lives in the present age, waiting for our blessed hope, the appearing of the glory of our great God and Savior Jesus Christ, who gave himself for us to redeem us from all lawlessness and to purify for himself a people for his own possession who are zealous for good works.

<u>PSALM 18:2-6</u> "The LORD is my rock, my fortress and my deliverer; my God is my rock, in whom I take refuge. He is my shield and the horn of my salvation, my stronghold. I call to the LORD, who is worthy of praise, and I am saved from my enemies. The cords of death entangled me; the torrents of destruction overwhelmed me. The cords of the grave coiled around me; the snares of death confronted me. In my distress I called to the LORD; I cried to my God for help. From his temple he heard my voice; my cry came before him, into his ears."

Time To Rise

Society teaches women-that their only weapon is to be sexually…
Because of this men are lacking what they need affectionately
A man can't be extraordinary-if we don't love them exceptionally
This confusion has caused our harmony & Unity to never meet perfectly

Society tells you lies, that your only worth what is between your thighs…
GOD said to be a leading lady because it is time for you to rise

Women it is our own fault-letting our men meet demise…
We made them hard to handle – by not hearing their cries.
We become objects of sex-because of our own character that dies
We allowed ourselves to only value- what is between our thighs.

You see Ladies-a man can't learn his greatness from a HOE
Only a woman of character and substance can help a man grow,
Women make men resent evil-when they are only after the dough…
And you were treated so ill –because you saw yourself that low.

Society tells you lies, that your only worth what is between your thighs…
GOD said to be a leading lady because it is time for you to rise

Women, live up to your essence of greatness and stop being used…
Stop hopping from bed to bed-like your changing your shoes..
Because you are to blame –if your worth nothing to loose,
And his actions are an excuse-for the trifling ways that you choose.

Women-we are the backbone-that can-make these men great.
Our gift can lift-no fakeness-no trip-if we just give and not take,
So stop running that game and all the bullshit that is so fake
By not lifting our men ….it is us that we break!!

Society tells you lies, that your only worth what is between your thighs…
GOD said to be a leading lady because it is time for you to rise

Women-know your value-see your most greatest potential
Having only a truthful word is such a valuable credential…
Know God's word –to walk in his spirit is exponential,
And to be GOD's leading lady is so very much essential.

My 12 Gauge

The World had locked me down- and I was in the devils cage…
But I was always Gods Poet - and now the world is my stage…
He Let me loose speaking in rhymes to display all my rage….
I kick truth, trigger the youth- my pens a 12 gauge
I once ran with thugs who sold drugs-did it all for that buzz,
Always looking over my shoulder waiting for the fuzz…
I used to write rhymes, snorting lines-now I am into different times,
Because God showed me hell and then said you are mine.
Had guns in my face- more than three times…should have been dead or close to flat line.
I became the backslider because church burned me with no love….
Said I don't want to struggle when I bling- bling –selling drugs…..
Plus I loved my crew and those sexy fine thugs…
And this Loud heavenly voice said "are you ready- your grave is already dug"
If you turn your back on my mercy, I am going to pull the plug.
You see my brain was black, from lacing blunts with crack….
God said "LET IT GO" because I am the need that you lack.
If you cannot hear then let me repeat that………
God said "LET IT GO" because I am the need that you lack.
So I let go of all those men who said " I Love you" in the sack..
And God made me into a soldier to take his world back!
I said but God…I am not soft-I grew up rough –rugged and raw…
I come from New York where they kick in the door waiving the 44
And God put the blood of Jesus-right on my kitchen floor,
And he showed me the cross like I had never seen before
Then he said "Is Your FAITH really that much of a chore?"
Or should I send you back to hell so that you can cry for me some more?
I am no longer locked down- because God broke my cage…
I am a prodigy from his grace-saving souls on stage
I pen lyrics that break yolks and the devil is enraged….
And the strongholds will come down but the war must wage..
I break satans back because the name of JESUS is my 12 gauge!

Struggle

Captivate a moment to sing out loud or dance
Remember life is filled with hopes and chance
Give your all in every type of circumstance
Be willing to risk on love and romance...
Learn about others and understand
Grasp the knowledge that is above all man
Help bring peace and extend your hand
Despite struggle, we are an extension of God's plan..
Life is what we all can carefully mold
Forget peoples' advice and what your told
Pray you will laugh when you get old
Be thankful for the priceless Grace we hold...
Dreams and wishes can be fulfilled
A bond of a family is what we build
Truth is an essence of what we willed
Fate met glory when our savior was killed...
Take a step up or a leap and bound
Make some loud noise or not a sound
Sometimes we can go round and round
but the soul is where your truly found...
Today you live and life you breathe
the web you found is what you weave
Materialism had so deceived...
Rejoice all the people who do believe
Sorrow will sometimes sweep you away
Speak your desire in the things you say
Remember every night to stop and pray
Tomorrow is the beginning to a better day
Let the past fade and the future begin
we all live in darkness and walk in sin
Don't let your brightness start to dim
We are made by the struggle and not the win.

Psalm 55:22 Cast thy burden upon the LORD, and he shall sustain thee: he shall never suffer the righteous to be moved.

Corporate America

Big Executives in nice suits-I call them sharks with a smile
They are as useless as their imported designer wall tile…
Expensive laptops, handcrafted mahogany desks they only sit at for a while.
What makes them look so smart is that working secretary going the extra mile.
Corporate America provokes an image of this clean cut working man…
If he is busy building a company than how did he get that awesome tan?
He is always out lunching and golfing because he knows all those women can
Get way deep in the trenches when the shit hits the fan…
Corporate America an advertisement of a man in a Versace suit,
The truth is when you work 10-15 hours a day you don't look that cute,
And women have been running your companies for too long staying mute.
So when you stand there smiling in accomplishment remember that we wear the boot.
Big Executives forget who is loyal, working late to make you great always with a smile.
We budget your business, expand your clients, keep in order every file…
And you treat us with no respect and that is what is so vile…
What will happen to you if we decide to stop living in such denial?
Corporate America makes us woman do way more than the description of our job.
Cell phones ringing, children screaming, your shirts dirty like a slob….
You are working deals and making meals as the boss vacations like a high class snob,
Then he presents your idea as his and you go home and sob.
The more valuable you become —the more that they expect…
The more you let them take your credit the less they show you respect
And you give your days and nights as from your family you disconnect.
You drag your sick kids to work because damn you need that check!
For that big bad boss- you go to extremes and exhaust yourself
And while you struggle to pay a bill- He expands an empire full of wealth.
You'll work from your bed and jeopardize your very own health
And as you break-only by you the pain will be felt….
Because Corporate doesn't owe you any help.
You are as replaceable as printer, how disgusting and despicable
They made you feel so needed but that is just predictable…
Corporate America has no conscious – no moral in money making
It is the forum we buy into and how we become so forsaking.

YOU LOST IT ALL...

You have lost it all including me ,a DUI again, asking me for money to lend
Drinking till 4 am doesn't bend, bringing you the worst results in the end
You have lost it all including me, it affected your job and you still pretend
Hate me for the truth, but if I do not help your issue than I am not a real friend

You have lost it all including me, and nothing mattered but that cold beer
You choose the alcohol, lie to all and make your own mother shed a tear
Nobody will address your addiction, but tough love should never ever fear
Because if I didn't step up to help you than you may not last another year...

You have free will to talk about me, say we fought about other crazy crap
But if the roles reversed and karma dispersed it, so equally in your lap...
It would be a very different story and it would be me who deserved a slap
But your mind can't rewind to comprehend how alcohol laid you on your back

But if the high and need makes you hurt people you love in so much disrespect
And loss of great things you now treat as if it meant nothing, in such neglect
Then damn you need to wake up and see that drinking has such an awful effect
But you think you got it controlled until you spiral down where your secret crept

You have lost it all including me ,a DUI again, asking me for money to lend
Drinking till 4 am doesn't bend, bringing you the worst results in the end
You have lost it all including me, it affected your job and you still pretend
Hate me for the truth, but if I do not help your issue than I am not a real friend

The functioning Alcoholic, popping pills prescribed for injuries that cause you pain
The obvious symptom of the disease is that you make everyone else to blame
Nobody makes you live up to your actions because enablers are tame...
And without all the support of those drinking buddies it wouldn't be the same

Sober would adjust your thinking ,get a mind clear from all that drinking
And what you would find is a lot of people's bullshit that is really stinking...
And stretching to reality where no medication is meddling in the proper linking....
May just bring you back to a conscious that is hiding behind that smile and winking

You have lost it all including me but you still don't see your own action
And when I addressed your problem, you said I yelled due to my own attraction
But I wanted to save your life not date a man with so much emotional infraction
Then you hide and lied because the truth of yourself will bring you no satisfaction

Whispers Of A Butterfly Warrior

You have lost it all including me ,a DUI again, asking me for money to lend
Drinking till 4 am doesn't bend, bringing you the worst results in the end
You have lost it all including me, it affected your job and you still pretend
Hate me for the truth, but if I do not help your issue than I am not a real friend

Daily Expressions

What we can be and what we are is so un-definable
Our Character and habits are very viable
For every word or way we present our self to God we are liable.
Our past is not our future, every moment has its grace,
God gave us life to cherish, to feel, to touch ,to taste.
Another beautiful day given to you ,is it really yours to waste,
the worlds definition of importance was given to you in haste.
They say success is measured by Surrender
Icons, false beliefs, tabs on the receiver or sender,
all this does is make us become a great pretender,
Don't fear to be yourself if God is your defender.
Be Strong like Job or Paul on Damascus Road,
Give God your life in faith be bold....
Don't induce your ego for your soul to be sold,
You are meant to be warmth in a world so cold

James 4:8 ....Come near to God and he will come near to you. Wash your hands, you sinners, and purify your hearts, you double-minded

Proverbs 27:17 ....As iron sharpens iron, so one man sharpens another.

Ecclesiastes 4:9-10 ....Two are better than one, because they have a good return for their work; If one falls down, his friend can help him up. But pity the man who falls and has no one to help him up,

Proverbs 13:20 .....He who walks with the wise grows wise, but a companion of fools suffers harms.

Whispers Of A Butterfly Warrior

Chapter Three:

Redemption In The Street

REDEEMER

The redeemer is the eternal light of life,
that shines through the darkness so bright.
The redeemer is the living water that we drink,
the conscience of our mind that makes us think.
The redeemer is the true vine, he is our Messiah,
He gives you inner peace that will take you higher.
He is the finisher of our faith, the father of our soul,
the one who judged you not and then made you whole.
He gave his flesh of self, he gave his only son,
but people kill each other with a click of a gun.
He gave you everything possible that he had to give,
and when you screwed it up he chose to forgive.
He is the redeemer, the only hope you have for grace,
the one who see's your beauty when no one see's your face.
He is the almighty redeemer the one who heals your wound,
he is the strength of salvation and the riser of the tomb.

Psalm 103:4 Who redeemeth thy life from destruction; who crowneth thee with lovingkindness and tender mercies;

Ephesians 1:7 In whom we have redemption through his blood, the forgiveness of sins, according to the riches of his grace.

Revelation 5:9 Thou wast slain, and hast redeemed us to God by thy blood

Whispers Of A Butterfly Warrior

Redemption for People in Pain:

I write in rhyme and give you food for thought thru poetry but now I am going to be raw like sand cutting the bottom of your feet-pain and pleasure is what we endure in the hot days....but life never gives you one without the other. The truth is I am a chameleon everywhere i go i can adapt. I became this way from a lack of self esteem... girls you know how you hit the college drinking circuit, then happy hour in corporate America and became reliant on liquid courage-Men you know that you size yourself up by women you conquer and measure your success in wealth and business instead of your soul. Chameleons do the same but use the mind to become whatever people want them to be, it is equal to the masks you wear in society so that nobody see's the real you because your all afraid that underneath that mask is someone nobody will like. Today ask yourself if you like you? Look in the mirror and see what looks back.?? We can never heal this generation of woman or men if we do not address the pain and sorrow that they are in. Your pain is aching, it is screaming out- you will not find the solution in the bottom of a liquor bottle or diet pills, the arms of another one night stand, becoming a workaholic, a pipe that feeds you false dreams. Why are women cutting their arms, sleeping with abusive men, overdosing, shopping addictively, and my biggest question is why do women feel the need to compete instead of uplift each other. Gossip and tear down each other instead of bond in friendship and be each other's rock! As a women I view this incredible anarchy amongst women and people that is sickening-I write to women and cry that they learn to value themselves more...yeah there are days when i feel like a void- no one listens- no one cares-that is the typical underlying emotional force that should drive you to become more aware that whatever you are doing must stop because Pain is GODS megaphone-and it will remain there until you decide to change- Ladies you are beautiful-decide today to become what GOD intended....perfume, worth more than rubies or gold, worth dying for....because that is just how GOD described you. Men decide to be the head of your household the role model, father to your children and protector to the weak. God made you so strong to be his warrior and strength in this world and sent his own son in that image...a misfit or failure but strive to be like Jesus and find the grace he sent to you because it is in front of you waiting to be found blinding every dark road you have chosen to stay on or choose to leave and turn from...........we choose and that is where we find our redemption.

1 John 4:18 There is no fear in love, but perfect love casts out fear. For fear has to do with punishment, and whoever fears has not been perfected in love.

Selfless Love

To love truly we must give up our self and tear down our own gratifications…
I could not understand myself being all worthy of a love of this sanctification,
Then I found myself praying on my knees for another one of Gods creations,
And praying for him to be blessed more than myself was a spiritual elevation.

I found myself hoping for his best and admiring his quirkiness and flaws….
Taking his pain into my own spirit and fighting for him when I had no cause.
Completely selfless and stripped of my flesh, my love had no end or pause
Just pure, raw emotional strength that broke all of those relationship laws….

I will forever be changed by knowing the man that I so prayed for at night….
He exists and is every characteristic that my heart longed for to be right.
I will wait for him in the darkness when cold lonely days cut me like a knife…
Because I never thought I would beg God to heal a man even if it meant take my life.

The selfless love I had only heard of as a myth just poured out of me like the rain….
Tugging my soul, aching to love him before myself was a love that is insane,
To want to give this man all of my blood, sweat, tears and ask for nothing in vain…
Surprised by my emotion I begged GOD to send someone better, despite my own pain.

Just knowing him has made me understand the capacity of GODs love a little more,
Because I cry when he seems broken and feel a sickness when his heart is tore,
To love a man as if he is a blessing from GOD to me and not another daily chore,
I will endure patience as I love him from a distance because I can feel him to my core….

No greater love in the flesh have I known, no selfless cries for another but this man,
That does not see or know the interceding prayer that put me to me knees as I ran…..
Never did I expect that I would love or adore him, because he was not in my plan,
And it was always him that GOD wanted me to love as selfless and gentle as lamb

And I do cry for him in prayer sometimes till my eyes begin to burn….
The respect for his inner beauty is something that I just feel, but could never learn
He is a man after GODs own heart and somehow my heart began to yearn….
And that selfless love that overwhelms my being will silently wait for my turn.

<u>1 Peter 4:8</u> Above all, keep loving one another earnestly, since love covers a multitude of sins.

POTTER AND CLAY

God is the potter and you are the clay
Don't be afraid of what people might say
You are a work of art in his hands today
God is always working and he will never go away.
God is the dayspring, redeemer, and bright morning star
Don't fight the hand that molds you into what you really are
Sometimes the clay might look disfigured, ruined or bizarre,
because he is not yet finished but has come very far.
You are a masterpiece in the making, beautifully designed
The lumps and dents shall fade into a shape newly defined
You are the figure he envisioned as he carefully creates,
a sculpture of his pride because he doesn't make mistakes.
Before the world had an ocean, the land had been laying dry
the sun was just a thought till God let it meet the sky
there were no green pastures or trees, until God said grow
and there was no running water till God told the river to flow.
God is the potter and you are the clay
Don't be afraid of what people might say
You are a work of art in his hands today
God is always working and he will never go away.
You are a fig that is desperate to become a tree
You are a sparrow in a cage waiting to be free
You are a lost child who is looking to be found
You are a rare rose, trying to break through the ground.
You are a vessel in the sea that must ride out the storm
because challenge and strain create for a better form
You are a seed in the Earth that will sprout in the spring
but you must battle the winter for what the sun will bring.
You are a broken tree branch with no use of good,
but Jesus is the carpenter and you are his wood
He smoothes the edges and sands the rough exterior
because he knows how something small can be made superior.

**Isaiah 64:8 But now, O LORD, You are our Father, We are the clay, and You our potter;
And all of us are the work of Your hand.**

GODS MISFIT

I am just a misfit to be used by GOD, like those in the Bible…
He brings me to your chaos to show you the holiness of his revival.
He uses my worst flaws, to drop the jaws of those who believe they are not libel.
He knows I am a misfit-but guides me with his angels to save those who are so vile.
I am a misfit, a pebble, a sinner, a human with my own test and trial…

John the Baptist was a misfit and like him I am a bit eccentric…
But his faith in his beheading made his message even more electric.
Rahab was an immoral prostitute and yet became so useful and effective.
Samson was co-dependant, Jeremiah depressed, Jonah reluctant but selective
Joseph was abused, Elijah was suicidal and Naomi was a widow so protective.

Moses stuttered and murdered but GOD spoke to him through a tree…
Gideon was poor, David had an affair and beat Goliath to set his people free.
Peter was hot tempered and impulsive but God said "walk on water with me"
Paul had poor health, Timothy was timid and Martha always worried of what would be,
And Zacchacus was unpopular but all of them had a purpose in the picture GOD could see.

GODS giants had the biggest issues and because of their faults they were of great use
Like the Samaritan woman, Bathsheba, Tamar or Ruth who was breaking laws of the jews,
You are chosen for his purpose and your brokenness will be a light he shall fuse….
You don't need to be perfect or amazing because he gives you all the tools….
He wrote it in his word and gave you the direction by commandments and his rules…

I am just a pebble and sometimes GOD throws me in the water to make a wave…
I am a vessel of GOD's and he drives my force to teach you before you hit the grave…
I am his misfit, a simple thought in his mind that he sets in motion for a soul to save.
A sinner that he uses anonymous in a world full of names that pave a way….
I am just a human, unworthy but ready to be used by him whenever he does say.

I am just a misfit, a pebble, a small part in a huge plan…..
A person, with mistakes and grace but covered by the blood of the lamb.
I am paralyzed by his glory, tell his story whenever I can…..
I am a misfit no different from every woman and every man,
I am just ready to be the warrior, and be used in his such perfect plan

Romans 5:20…But where sin abounded, grace abounded much more…

Single Fathers-Men Of Faith

Humble man you are every woman's desire and every mans envy of being
Because you exalt masculinity while standing tall in what they are seeing...
You stand your ground, with your kids you play around, and you speak truthfully sound.....
Not waiving for praise because in the kingdom of heaven you will wear a royal crown....

Handsome single father left all alone and for his children he won't deceive......
down on his hands and kness in prayer because he has the will to still believe,
Praying for his children and trying not to grieve for the one who chose to leave
God restores what locust have eaten just keep planting that seed....

Society and worldly standards say men are strong and should not cry...
But your greatest compassion is learned thru the tears in your eye
A greater love is known when another love dies..
only you can mentor those children to stand up and rise.
They learned your moral integrity when you protected them from the lies...

You stepped up and like a legend you embraced all of the struggles and pain...
The 10 hour work days, dinners, baths, homework, class snack to correctly train...
Raising them up in the way of the Bible in a world full of so much insane
Bed Time stories, the flu, forgotten books at school and you never complain.
Man of Faith your sacrafices for these children will never be in vain!

You may have felt broken but your actions were complete,
strong and everything a man should be in this life
Your an unmeasured blessing to our future letting God take the Lead in your strife...
Your amazing and unforgettable to me in a world so badly torn apart,
Because you are an example of a man after God's own heart.

70 Percent of people who commit suicide are from fatherless homes while 80 percent of inmates, violent offenders and addicts possess the same link of not having a male role model or presence in the home to guide or teach them.

The Mask You Wear

Would it be so horrible to remove that mask you wear every day?
The one you put on when you are what everyone wants, in what you do and say?
The hard shell, that surrounds your softest, most loving, generous way?
The mask that hides the best version of you and decomposes it like decay…

The mask that makes you the hardcore bitch boss ,because softness doesn't sell.
The irony of pretending to be below others when you could crack their very shell,
The shell that keeps the caged bird in it's place when its freedom is a story to tell.
The bondage you experience everyday that keeps you in the rat race of hell!

Rip it off, toss it, throw it off the high rise terrace and just take the plunge and leap,
The bigger the success you can be comes from the fast free falls depth so steep…
You have worn that mask and made it pretty but the beauty within is buried too deep.
No longer can you pretend or hide the amazing parts of you they make you put to sleep!

Hide your unique expression and make the most important impression…
We are taught this and later it becomes a catatonic loss and expensive lesson.
We conform our mask into what others decide and loose our personal blessing…
And spend years trying to dig it back up on a counselors couch in session.

Ironic it is that the very person we suppress is the person we were meant to be,
But the mask makes it so much easier to stand tall and be firm like a tree…
Because society teaches us that being different is something we don't like to see,
Yet every commercial emphasizes this perfect American Family in the land of the free

We no longer exercise freedom of speech or make a radical work of art,
Instead we wear that suit and push corporate America's financial cart…
And tomorrow morning we will put on the mask and do it all again to be smart,
And a little more we will forget the person under the mask for a new start.

Would it be so horrible to remove that mask you wear every day?
The one you put on when you are what everyone wants, in what you do and say?
The hard shell, that surrounds your softest, most loving, generous way?
The mask that hides the best version of you and decomposes it like decay…

Psalm 56:11 In God have I put my trust: I will not be afraid what man can do unto me.

You Make Me feel....

There are not enough words in the world to express the way I feel
When I am safe within your arms and know that you are real…
I find peace in our conversation and pleasure in your hands touch
You fill me with compassion and your voice makes my heart begin to rush

You make me feel more loved than anyone or anything…..
I can't believe that when you are near the laughter and smile you bring
You make me feel beautiful, as if I need to do nothing to be whole
You lift the light of my life and it shines out to the surface from my soul.

You say all the right things and I remember every word…
You take the time to listen, when I am needing to be heard.
You give me the affection with your eyes that any woman would desire
You elevate my mind and make me want to excel thru a conscious that is higher.

You look at me with fondness and love me with your eyes…
You are my best friend because your honesty will never tell lies.
You make me see that huge mountain as smaller in size…
Because you believe I can achieve and then make me realize….

You make me feel empowered, you stand back and let me be strong…
You let me roar like a lion even when I am doing something wrong .
You make me feel free to be me when I am silly like a love song,
But you let me be that fragile woman who needs you when I mourn.

You stand back and let my unique qualities embrace my being…
And when I conquer my battle, you smile at the qualities your seeing.
Your ability to love my faults and laugh at my quirkiness is totally freeing,
And when the tears are flowing down your kindness is where I am leaning.

You make me feel complete and cherished beyond any words description…
You smooth every edge of roughness and blend into my world's friction
You make me feel respected and loved when the environment shows affliction.
You are the words of love on a wall when I could not read the encryption.

<u>1 John 4:8</u> Anyone who does not love does not know God, because God is love.

<u>1 Corinthians 16:14</u> Let all that you do be done in love.

<u>1 Corinthians 13:1 – 13</u> If I speak in the tongues of men and of angels, but have not love, I am a noisy gong or a clanging cymbal. And if I have prophetic powers, and understand all mysteries and all knowledge, and if I have all faith, so as to remove mountains, but have not love, I am nothing. If I give away all I have, and if I deliver up my body to be burned, but have not love, I gain nothing. Love is patient and kind; love does not envy or boast; it is not arrogant or rude. It does not insist on its own way; it is not irritable or resentful; ...

It Only Takes One

They say that it only takes one snowflake to start an avalanche,
He is the very vine of the tree and we are his branch…
They say it only takes one soldier, one bullet and one gun,
If you have the power to change this world than why do you run?
It only takes one voice to start a protest but you are afraid to speak,
No wonder the world is going to hell when people become too weak.
It only takes one death to plague one million by an airborne disease,
It only takes one ozone layer to fade away and to death we will freeze.
It only takes one dose of anthrax to kill thousands of marines…
As our government signs one bill that medicates our junkie fiends.
We build methadone clinics and Unemployment starts to rise…
It only took one minuet for an earthquake to take 20,000 lives…
A tsunami develops and it is only by one massive wave….
And families and villages are sent by water to an early grave.
The Twin Towers falling started with only one commercial plane,
And the Typhoon that killed so many started with just a little rain.
You can make a difference, you can be the change in society,
You can be the person of GOD who brings people back sobriety.
You can be an example or just the hand of compassion,
That leads to make a difference in a world ruled by ego bashin.
An idea can start a movement, a conversation created a war
And if there is one like you others will follow thru the door…
It only takes one act of kindness to change another life…
And one act of evil to be the hand that held the knife.
There is power in one person and power in one voice….
You are an army of one, so today please make that choose.

Necessary Edification

Stripped of our Ego, we are burned by our very fleshly self and bone,
A process of renewal so painful to endure that you may scream or groan
Seeping out like an infection our own impure wounds open that were not sown
A spreading virus in your soul that must be conquered by you and GOD alone

Cleansing all the rotten, immobilizing and paralyzing you it must be purged
Burnt down like an offering on an alter inside killing your senses every nerve
Toxic spreading no more letting it deform you like a strait molecule in curve
Defining and clarifying all the realigning that will take every sinful thought you urge

Emancipate all the daggers piercing a heart that must become a new creation
Rip the steel, skin will heal, but remaining with it will cripple your path to elevation
To become a diamond, a piece of coal must sustain the high heat of all purification
But when its clean with no darkness in between it becomes a beautiful eye sensation
And from just coal mines of dirt, wipe the hurt and become the worthy expectation
Because to get his grace you must place yourself through GOD's Necessary Edification

The even smallest envies need to bleed and burn you so you will never lead
The wrong desires can be like wildfires and won't take you higher to your creed
And many people push you to anger or exiled danger that you cannot impede
Because the slightest sin, dishonest win, arrogant prideful grin is the wrong seed
And you must edify every lie that makes you cry so your actions and words are freed

Triumph is not the goal but to conquer all that pulls you and wrongfully entices
The little things that slowly stings but grow into huge stumbling blocks called vices
The people who pain and the ego so vain that lead you to a boat that just capsizes
The bad attitude or being in judgment so rude that you can't renew so it paralyzes
And the power you gave to just be a slave because you were unwilling to sacrifices

Emancipate all the daggers piercing a heart that must become a new creation
Rip the steel, skin will heal, but remaining with it will cripple your path to elevation
To become a diamond, a piece of coal must sustain the high heat of all purification
But when its clean with no darkness in between it becomes a beautiful eye sensation
And from just coal mines of dirt, wipe the hurt and become the worthy expectation
Because to get his grace you must place yourself through GOD's Necessary Edification

Four Horsemen of the Apocalypse

GOD said to "Fear none of those things which thou shall suffer in my name"...
Nations will rise against nations, the four horsemen will come but your faith must remain.
His warning to protect, bless Israel and hurt not the oil or the wine is written very plain...
His text of Revelation describes that the apocalypse must come and nothing will be the same.

Will you be one of the 144,000 left in this world to survive the pestilence and disease?
The White horse of Conquest will appear as a false prophet and in him will you believe?
The Red horse is named War and he represents the blood we will spill over to grieve....
The black horse is the famine, draught, mass starvation that will kill the crops leaves.

The fourth horse is the pale green one and his name is death as he brings imminent decay.
Stars will fall from the sky and no moon will light the night and no sun will be seen in the day.
Abomination causes desolation and in this time the antichrist will rise in our world to play...
The church will be defiled and compromised by the unclean hearts that falsify GOD and pray.

The seven trumpets will sound with the breaking of the seven seals opened by the lamb...
And destruction of great Earthquakes will shake the core of Earth to be felt by every land.
One third of the humankind will die by judgment for the evil participation they plan....
And the seas will turn to blood as plagues will soar your bodies to be bridle as the sand.

Some of us who just play church will just be cast by the Angels in a lake of fire....
Some will be devoured by your very own bad addictions, words or desires.
We will believe we are untouchable by Armageddon because the devil is a liar,
But the word of GOD is very clear about the coming of our great Messiah......

We are warned of the dragon, the whore of Babylon and the mark of the beast....
We are told the rules and commandments to be warriors of GOD who will not cease.
We are taught external punishment in hell where on your own flesh you feast....
So why are we holding the hand of damnation by our very actions to say the least.

PSALM 18:32-38
"It is God who arms me with strength and makes my way perfect. He makes my feet like the feet of a deer; he enables me to stand on the heights. He trains my hands for battle; my arms can bend a bow of bronze. You give me your shield of victory, and your right hand sustains me; you stoop down to make me great. You broaden the path beneath me, so that my ankles do not turn."

Gravity To My Soul

When I am around you, it is like the gravity in my soul tugging forward uncontrollable,
And the thought of my lips touching yours but being able to stop would be deceivable.

Because if I were to touch you in that way I may never come back from euphoric bliss
Afraid because, you would become the only man in this world that I would want to kiss.

Fear that I could not control the temptation or deny myself from your touch….
Yet not wanting you to know that your effect on me is overpowering me this much.

You are like gravity to my soul pulling the core of my being directly to your path….
Over and over again and as I try to resist becomes more of an unbearable aftermath

Like two souls searching for each other blinded by our own reason beyond any time,
As our connection is greater than the lapse we created and the force is so divine….

Created perfectly to fit together as if something that was just meant to be tightly entwined,
And no matter how hard we fight this feeling, I continue to cross your path as you do mine

No longer fighting this attraction, because I feel that if I do not touch you I will die…..
And denying the gravity to my soul that you have makes me so sick that I could cry.

Dreaming, at night until I do not want to sleep as my unconscious screams your name..
And to not see you or hear your voice is like a jagged unsteadiness that just brings me pain.

Then there are those moments that I cannot breathe from the simple thought of you,
And I cannot fathom that this intense ache or emotional attraction could be this true….

Your essence surrounds me from afar and calls my spirit like a connected vine…
And like two lights in the dark frantically searching for each other the stars will align

You are like an extension of inner being, that got lost or detached, without it not whole…

No matter how I repress the desire I cannot let go because you are the gravity to my soul.
Colossians 2:2 That their hearts may be encouraged, being knit together in love, to reach
all the riches of full assurance of understanding and the knowledge of God's mystery,
which is Christ.

JUST LET GO

Let go of that man, don't worry how you hurt, what he said or who he is sleeping with
Let go of the bondage from self hate you create that keeps you from your destined gift
Let go of trying to make other people happy as you continue to love, respect and give
Let go of trying to help those people who won't own up to the actions they chose to live

Let go of that disease to be like the rest of the crowd that strive to people please
Let go of trying to force harmony with people in trauma and drama that need to leave
Let go of other peoples self lies that they absorb into cries but choose life that denies
Let go of comforting those people who cynically pull out all of your bonds of love ties

Let go of trying to make other people face their own vices or face up to a problem
Let go of thinking you can change a person or make them see how to solve them…
Let go of your own delusion or façade that makes you pretend pain you do not feel
Let go of thinking that if you avoid it and don't face it down than it will be less real

Let go of that urge for bittersweet revenge or idea you can teach someone a lesson
Let go of trying to understand how other people crap all over their own succession
Let go and just let GOD, let go and move toward a greatness inside that will achieve
Let go and just let GOD do what he does and move in your life when you do believe.

JOHN 14:27 Peace, I leave with you, my peace I give unto you: not as the world giveth, give I unto you. Let not your heart be troubled, neither let it be afraid.

Luke 17:3-4 So watch yourselves. "If your brother sins, rebuke him, and if he repents, forgive him. If he sins against you seven times in a day, and seven times comes back to you and says, 'I repent,' forgive him."

PROVERBS 18:10 …The name of the LORD is a strong tower; the righteous run to it and are safe.

Scarlet Letter

No Matter how much I change or how hard I struggle and climb high enduring in stride,
You remind me of every mistake I ever made, keeping those memories burning alive….
No Matter what good I do or how many lives I touch or people I could save….
You hold up my regrets and show me wrong choices from the past that I have made.
Your judge and jury of me is no good and your voiced out opinion pushes me to the wall,
Unconditional love does not persecute you when you are recovering from a long fall….
No Matter how GOD can use me, all you want to see is my past like a big scarlet letter
And you detour me from my greatness and define what you believe makes me better…..
People try to mold me, GOD try's to hold me and I suffocate from the grip of your hand,
But all I needed was for you to accept and love me even when you could not understand…..
Some days I just want to slip into the darkness and forget what you all want me to be,
Because people keep wrapping me into bondage that keeps me from flying so free….
People want to help me but hinder the very essence that sets me apart from all the rest,
And it was those battles I lost and obstacles I faced all alone that still bring forth my very best.
No matter how far I go or what love I give to you, you still see my past or red scarlet letter,
But someday you will see how necessary it was in my journey and how it made me so much better.
My wounds were meant to help others overcome, my pain was meant for compassion I learn,
My paths and roads have lessons undefined and bridges that you just cannot burn…..
Because I live by the sword, die by my pen and finally found I have nothing left to pretend,
Because one day I woke up all alone and realized that nobody was truly my friend…….
So I slip away in your echo of confusion and that caring part of me slowly disappears
Because I now put forth boldness in the dream of who I am and not those rejected tears.
So it does not matter what you think I should do or how you hold that red scarlet letter…..
Because everything you judged in me was what GOD used to elevate me into someone better.

JOB 11:16 Thou shalt forget thy misery, and remember it as waters that pass away.
ROMANS 8:1 There is therefore now no condemnation for those who are in Christ Jesus.

Whispers Of A Butterfly Warrior

MY WINGS, MY WAY

Where are my wings and when will they help me learn to fly…
Will I ever make the difference in this world before I lay down to die?
Where are my wings and when will they help me learn to fly…
Will my lessons learned leave a legacy to those who think GOD is a lie?

My wings feel broken, my heart bruised and my soul stolen….
From the darkness of so many hard ego's that stay swollen.
The deep water is murky but my oars of faith keep on rowing …
And when my arms are heavy then Jesus does most the towing.

I am a survivor, a prodigal and stubborn to do things my way,
So many times God threw me the lifeline in the words he did say.
No matter my pride or own will his unconditional love did stay.
And no matter the sin I committed his shelter over me did not fray.

Where are my wings and when will they help me learn to fly…
Will I ever make the difference in this world before I lay down to die?
Where are my wings and when will they help me learn to fly…
Will my lessons learned leave a legacy to those who think GOD is a lie?

No matter what the devil sends to destroy me, God unravels his plan,
The perfect, unique masterpiece painted thru a tornado, like only he can.
The grace in my mental torment and blessings beyond the hurricane on land
A higher power that destructs all the weapons formed against me by man.

Because being different or special and talented feels like a curse to carry…
Living in your destiny walking a broken road and believing is scary….
A purpose driven mind bent to be like everyone, susceptible to ordinary…
Trying not to stand out doing it my way when my path is to be extraordinary.

Where are my wings and when will they help me learn to fly…
Will I ever make the difference in this world before I lay down to die?
Where are my wings and when will they help me learn to fly…
Will my lessons learned leave a legacy to those who think GOD is a lie?

Before I met Christ

Before I met Christ, I was lost and unable to see
I was living my life like I thought it should be
I never saw potential or promise to break free
I never knew the goodness that was dormant in me

I was sad, lonely, seriously depressed…..
Nobody ever told me GOD chose us to be blessed.

Bitterness was a feeling that was easy to conceive,
Everyone treated others the way they were deceived…
I wish I had known how to be the heart that believed.

When I reached out to others, they didn't have the time…
But when those friends came to me I made them feel fine.

Everyday my heart broke and a piece of me did die..
I smiled and joked like I was happy but it was all a lie.

Life was so negative and my hurt and pain did rule.
Then one day I woke up and realized that I was the fool,

I saw Christ on a cross ,I saw his hand pinned by a nail,
I wondered about all the times I had settled to fail.

I saw the whip marks on his back and thorns in his head.
I cried at the thought, of all the times I wished I was dead.

I saw the blood he had shed as it dripped from his skin.
I realized the purpose of my life was to not always win.
So I started all over and asked GOD to take away my sin…
He gave me a new road and another chance to to again begin.

Before I met Christ, I had low self esteem and many fears.
Then I overcame an addiction that –held me down for years
.

I was trapped in a desert with no water and no air.
I was surrounded by fake people who really didn't care.
But Christ gave me back my breath in the cross he did bare
.

I learned to find victory in the pain that life may bring to you.
I learned to still love and help those who are not so true.

I learned to forgive all the evil and lend my hand to give,
I learned what it meant again to laugh, love and live….

I learned to find Gods power when I felt so weak,
I found strength to not avenge and finally became meek.

I learned that a person's character is the greatest possession,
And those who do not have it, will eventually learn that lesson.

I found peace in a storm and rainbows of promise in the cloud,
I found a lucid silence in a world so overbearingly loud….

I found my way out of darkness and back into the light,
I found that Christ would give endurance to a path that is right.

I plead like Jarius on the trail or like Joseph at the table….
That you join me in the walk as your welcome to GODS table.

Job 16:20 "My friends scorn me: but mine eye poureth out tears unto God."
Isaiah 35:4 … say to those with fearful hearts, "Be strong, do not fear; your God will come, he will come with vengeance; with divine retribution he will come to save you.
Psalm 23 "The LORD is my shepherd; I shall not want. He maketh me to lie down in green pastures: he leadeth me beside the still waters. He restoreth my soul: he leadeth me in the paths of righteousness for his name's sake. Yea, though I walk through the valley of the shadow of death, I will fear no evil: for thou art with me; thy rod and thy staff they comfort me. Thou preparest a table before me in the presence of mine enemies: thou anointest my head with oil; my cup runneth over. Surely goodness and mercy shall follow me all the days of my life: and I will dwell in the house of the LORD for ever."

MAKE ME NEW

Lord make me new, let them see you…
Let your word be seen in everything I speak and do
Let the label be stripped and make me your tool,
Let them see the miracle that I see so true.

Lord make me into the person I was designed to be,
Free me from the bondage of this world-let me be free.
Like a blind man, you opened my eyes to see
That my purpose is found, in the nail of that tree.

His brow dripped with blood –pierced by a crown of thorns
He has given you deliverance and his book of law warns,
That you do not idolize, criticize, patronize those he mourns
For he is salvation against the predator with deadly horns
And if you know his grace than you know how he scorns

Lord let me be a light to darkness, when all else fails,
Let me take on the cross because I choose your nails,
Let me be your feet washer, or a servant washing chairs.
Because you remain my salvation, even when nobody cares.

He is my salvation, redemption, light, alpha & omega, and all between
He is my father, my husband , best friend and my lord and I am his queen…
I am a treasure he wants to bless from the prodigal journey on him I lean
Because, he made me a soldier and from hell I am redeemed.

Lord make me new, let them see you…
Let your word be seen in everything I speak and do
Let the label be stripped and make me your tool,
Let them see the miracle that I see so true.

Ecclesiastes 3:11 "He has made everything beautiful in its time"

Matthew 8:2 And behold, a leper came to him and knelt before him, saying, "Lord, if you will, you can make me clean."

Whispers Of A Butterfly Warrior

World Changer -Soul Saver

You are a world changer- a soul saver...a servant of God doing hard labor
You reach out to the lost souls, coworkers, associates and neighbors...
Not following the crowd but being your own road paver...
Fighting the strongholds and mindsets of evil to find GOD's favor.

You must be purified like Gold and be refined by the fire...
Your chaos and pain incubate a birth and the devil is a liar...
Embrace and rejoice in a defeated moment because it will retire,
Your troubles came to transform you to take you much higher.

People may not even see you in the running or list you as a contender,
A higher power already see's you there because he is your sender...
Destiny is delivered to you in your difficulty, so you must always remember,
The turmoil and long suffering is in the mighty name of your defender.

You are in a temporary season to receive a permanent blessing...
The harder the cries-the bigger the prize for all of your stressing,
Hit your knees, roll up your sleeves and start the confessing...
Because the King needs you to fight and there is no resting.

Tell them he is coming- don't let them live in such deceit...
Be GOD's Noble Warrior –for those souls-even if you get beat.
Stand strong and don't let them rape you of your belief.....
Because the only moment that matters is when you and GOD meet
And your freedom of speech still stands when they knock you off your feet!

You are a world changer- a soul saver...a servant of God doing hard labor
You reach out to the lost souls, coworkers, associates and neighbors...
Not following the crowd but being your own road paver...
Fighting the strongholds and mindsets of evil to find GOD's favor.

Matthew 12:36,37
But I tell you that men will have to give account on the day of judgment for every careless word they have spoken. For by your words you will be acquitted, and by your words you will be condemned.

THE MUSTARD SEED

A small mustard seed is all you need but sometimes it gets cracked,
People can defeat you and sometimes you will feel trapped....
In the empty wasteland of this life in a corner you are backed,
But God said that little seed is the faith you need in what is lacked.
The mustard seed, small as a particle of dust or a coffee bean,
The simplest form of his promise to hold onto your dream...
The little piece of God when you have no where else to lean,
The hope in your exhausted state, that there is more than what is seen.
Cracked, crushed, bent, distorted the mustard seed will remain,
Like the knowing, that GOD is with you, through all of this pain...
When it is still, quiet, movement free and the future seems lame,
Just like GOD, the mustard seed does not change but stays the same.
So small and delicate but like a rock that does not break...
Something real you cannot see but make no mistake....
The seed holds all you need when all else in this world is fake.
You do not need a mountain or a cup but just a seed is all it will take.
This little seed of faith parted the red sea, set people free,
So have you asked yourself what does it have for me?
It is the promise of things you cannot see for what will be...
It is so small to you but to him it is already an oak tree.
You are to be his soldier, with your seed a faithful ornament,
Hold onto that seed even when others don't see it is significant
It is the promise of your life that will take you to magnificent...
His Majesty said not to follow them but choose to be the different
A small mustard seed is all you need but sometimes it gets cracked,
People can defeat you and sometimes you will feel trapped....
In the empty wasteland of this life in a corner you are backed,
But God said that little seed is the faith you need in what is lacked.

Matthew 17:20
**If ye have faith as a grain of mustard seed, ye shall say unto this mountain, Remove
hence to yonder place; and it shall remove; and nothing shall be impossible unto you.**

Whispers Of A Butterfly Warrior

BELIEVE IN THE SILENCE

There are many obstacles in our way-we need to overcome and let go…
The only way of healing-is to allow Gods ever present spirit to flow,
Maybe someone hurt you, or you felt the wrath of a lying tongue,
Remember the battle is not yours-it is the God of justices-and he has already won.
He has given us the blood of the lamb and great testimony to overcome….
He has given us the breastplate of righteousness-a promise our prayers are done.

There are many mountains to climb-which might make you feel weak,
But you can glide to the top because the Lord gives you hinds feet.
He asks us to have faith-he has told us to become humble and meek.
He has given us eternal life-but it is his face we must diligently seek.
For the top of the mountain is high-but we will go on -past it's peak!

I know we all have times when we ask "God Where Are You?"
Yet he never seems to fail us- because he always brings us through
When we are falling apart inside-his mercy becomes our glue…
He never forgot a servant-a warrior who has struggled-to stay true
And he never forgets his promise-to make our heart become new

We think we can fix the problem or -that we can become clever
But without Gods will and purpose —our plan to conquer becomes a never
And our pain becomes overwhelming-and sorrow feels like it lasts forever,
But remember Gods love and plan- is a chord we cannot sever…..

When the world echoes with hatred and you only see life's dreary gloom.
Remember Jesus cried "Where are you God ?" and was risen from the tomb
Think of Abraham's promise-after thirty years God filled his wife's womb.
Remember John the Baptist facing death in a dungeon-but his faith was not consumed.
Let Go and let God be your strength-and his answers will come to you soon.

Many times in life, you will fail and feel like your stuck in a bottomless pit
Then recall how Jesus healed a blind man with just some dirt and spit….
We shall be like gentle lambs of God-our faith shall keep us quiet and calm
David said he trusted, relied on and was confident in the Lord- in the 31st psalm,
Just like Jesus still believed so strong-when the nail entered in his palm

God's Boomerang

As a child I believed I was dumb because I was dyslexic with disability in learning
But as an Adult I became a Deans list honor student because I had a yearning…

As a teen pothead laughing at speeches warning me a gateway to drugs was weed
I lost years of my life in crack to become an interventionist with compassion to lead

As a fat kid who had to be funny because popular kids laughed at my double chin
I became a beautiful adult with amazing revolt to teach GOD made and chose your skin

Every situation can be turned around by the power of GOD's boomerang
He restores what the locust have eaten and our amazing grace will be sang
Every evil the devil sent to hurt you was interceded by GOD's boomerang
He makes crooked paths strait and lifts us off the destructive noose we hang

As a person who thought of suicide as a way out and was lost in all desperation
I became an advocate for better mental health that can provide you elevation

As a welfare mother who could not survive and struggled to put food in the fridge
I endured as a Survivor who is fierce and knows every obstacle is your next bridge…

As a physically assaulted woman I was crushed in spirit and lost all hope to believe
But as a woman of Christ who chose a new life I teach that mindset will deceive

Every situation can be turned around by the power of GOD's boomerang
He restores what the locust have eaten and our amazing grace will be sang
Every evil the devil sent to hurt you was interceded by GOD's boomerang
He makes crooked paths strait and lifts us off the destructive noose we hang

As a girl with low self esteem I encountered the power of mean verbal abuse
I Educate you in integrity and negative was free from all labels we choose to refuse

As a bar hopping party girl, in the social single whirl, I encountered sex we call rape
I protest the violent act, but never the less attack the injury we bandage with tape…

As a dependant of liquid courage, only bold by alcohol with no real friend to call
I teach people that sobriety enlarges life to engage people not so shallow and small

Every situation can be turned around by the power of GOD's boomerang
He restores what the locust have eaten and our amazing grace will be sang
Every evil the devil sent to hurt you was interceded by GOD's boomerang
He makes crooked paths strait and lifts us off the destructive noose we hang

I Lay you at the Alter

I lay you at the alter, I lay you at the cross....
My tears weep like the willows calling to the moss.
I lay you at the alter, I lay you at the cross
My prayers break yolks like the waves crashing as they toss.
My eyelids are heavy, exhausted by your burdens and pains...
I pray for all your blessings and pray for your gain.
My soul is tormeneted, as you cry out for my help...
Unravel the ropes, chained like seaweed and sticking like kelp.
I lay you at the alter, I lay you at the cross...
Blood was shed all over so your soul would not be a loss..
Salty water stinging the open wounds, and for help you will scream,
his arms are wide open , he gives you the stability to lean...
Drowning in your sin, suffocating and your lungs gasping for air
I pray for your atonement in the crosses you bear.
I lay you at the alter, I lay you at the cross....
My tears weep like the willows, calling to the moss
This is your huge spiritual mountain, so get up and start to climb,
Put your fingers in the dirt and dig your heals in and grind.
Grasp your hands on that rope till they bleed,don't quit,don't fall
It may be huge for you but for God this task is nothing at all..
I lay you at the alter, I lay you at the cross....
My prayers break yokes like the waves crashing as they toss.
Fully explore & expose your weakness, so God can make you strong.
the road may be caving in, but it won't be that long.
He is your rock, the messiah that says to seek his face
He is the forgiveness that you need to so embrace.
I lay you at the alter, I lay you at the cross....
My tears weep like the willows, calling to the moss.
I lay you at the alter, I lay you at the cross..
My prayers break yolks like the waves crashing as they toss

ROMANS 3:23 For all have sinned and fall short of the glory of God.

SHIFT

I am a victim, a human being that will naturally then victimize
A product of my environment by default and yet I cannot recognize
That the law of Karma and attraction is a power that never lies
And you enhance what you give attention to, even if it's what we despise

I never wanted this to be me…and I really didn't want to see
What comes around goes around and it all came back on me…
Because everything you give or take creates a ripple of energy
So be careful what do or say and visualize everything peacefully

Every cruel word I said, wrote to be read or thought in my head
Made me feel anguish so deep that I wanted it over, buried and dead
Because the law of the universe knows nothing but what it is fed
And hell, it doesn't feel good when it lays back down in your bed…

So SHIFT your vibration, speak prosperity and abundance to all
And when violence attacks your being bring anger to a crawl
Reaction is no surprise but negative vibration, take down to small
And see the very change you made against conflict that looked so tall

I am now light and love reflective, like a ball in full positive bounce
Because I know what you weigh in thought you physically pronounce
So back away from hate and identify it to be constructive and renounce
And every vibration in emotional action flows back to you by the ounce…

So SHIFT your element of vibration to an amazing gratitude
Being thankful for every bad thing not returning comments spewed
And shift a conversation to harmony even if it began so harsh or rude
And every negative law you can change by transforming what we elude

Do not run from conflict because then you give it a power to own
And face it with a belief it will be better and teach us as we've grown
If you fear something then you intensify facing that giant all alone
Because the law you did not SHIFT and by attention you have now sewn

So SHIFT and give kindness to those, who really do not deserve
Because it is like taking on a fastball and spinning it with a curve
And if something can annoy you and attention is on your very last nerve
Because you empowered it by complaining instead of giving it a swerve

Chapter Four

Concrete Ashes from a Blinding light

Beauty For Ashes

God gives beauty for ashes to all cultures divine.
God knows the believers who will overcome the swine.
You're everyday angels, not a branch but the very vine.
Without you ,is to have communion without the wine.
You are my people who teach compassion that cannot decline.
You are the promise of tomorrow, bringing more hope to shine.
You shall not be scared of death, you are immortal to time.
You are my chosen child ,your life is in the hands of mine.
Beauty for your ashes and I bring smiles for your pain.
I am the sunshine glowing through after the rain.
Beauty for your ashes and healing to your wounds.
I am the silence you find in loudness that consumes.
Beauty for your ashes and sleep for your deprivation.
I am the water for your thirst, to fulfill your dehydration.
You have the blood of the lamb and testimony to overcome.
Wear the breastplate and I promise, prayers are done.
Beauty for your ashes and peace for your struggle within.
Stripes upon my back so you heal from the flesh of your skin.
Grace and forgiveness so you could be clean to again begin.
My son's life on a cross for everyday you have lived in sin.

Isaiah 61:3...To give them beauty for ashes, the oil of joy for mourning, the garment of praise for the spirit of heaviness...

Whispers Of A Butterfly Warrior

Never Good Enough

I wonder why God would want me to hear how I am "Not Good Enough"
But he made her my family so my skin would wear thin, only to be tough
There is a purpose in his plan I must remember, because this pain is rough
But my endurance to tolerate her bitterness is conquering all thru his love

I mop her floors at 5am,clean the dishes and couches after a 10 hour work day
I honor her like the bible and cry to find love or sympathy for her when I pray
But the moment I walk in the house and before I can get in my bed and lay
She wounds me like daggers of words by an insult or degrades me in her way

I am "Never Good Enough" and she hates the way I clean her cups and plates
She says I use too much Lysol and while I do laundry she informs or berates
And goodness, I cook too spicy and all the meals I make she completely hates
and either I need to get out of the house or she criticizes all of my first dates

And I am "Never Good Enough" because of what I did in my wild past
And every day I pay by hearing what I do wrong and comments with sass
So I stay at the office later to inspire my team but I get home and it won't last
Because the arsenal of insults are always waiting at the door to hit me fast…

I wonder why God would want me to hear how I am "Not Good Enough"
But he made her my family so my skin would wear thin only to be tough
There is a purpose in his plan I must remember, because this pain is rough
But my endurance to tolerate her bitterness is conquering all thru his love

I can't raise my children correctly if I am at the office more than home
And even if I call to check on her I get an attitude thru the phone
Yet I will run her errands, cut her toe nails that are fully overgrown
And she always gets the last word even if her true colors are shown

She manipulates the situation and always turns everything around
And GOD forbid you prove yourself, mind correct your world hits the ground
Because she will make life a daily living hell with every dirty looking frown
And the worst thing I did to her life was get a clear conscious that was sound

I wonder why God would want me to hear how I am "Not Good Enough"
But he made her my family so my skin would wear thin, only to be tough
There is a purpose in his plan I must remember, because this pain is rough
But my endurance to tolerate her bitterness is conquering all thru his love

IF I SHALL LEAVE THIS EARTH

If I shall ever find my time has come to leave this earth.
I pray God is satisfied with the things I have done since birth.

If I should die before I awake, then I leave a part of me to live.
God gave me a blessed life so like him in my death, I shall give.

I would want my sense of touch to be given to one who cannot feel.
I want my fearless faith to go to a person they say cannot heal.

I want my tender heart put in a person who is cynical and mean.
I want my smile to grace a deformed face that has never gleamed.

The end could be coming but nobody should fear to die,
Instead you should brace yourself to learn how to fly.

Some people learn this on earth and then some may never find,
That sweet gentle love that cannot be lost with time.

If I should die before I awake, give my eyes to one who can't see.
Let my ashes be put in the earth to soil the most beautiful tree.

I am ready to give my outspoken words to one who cannot talk.
I am ready to trade in my legs to a cripple who may finally walk.

God is with us every day and he can be your strength through disease.
God is ready, willing, able and he is there for your pain to be eased,

With God there is nothing that can hurt you and nothing ye shall fear.
For I am glad God blessed me with life and that he is calling me near.

<u>Philippians 3:8</u> **Indeed, I count everything as loss because of the surpassing worth of knowing Christ Jesus my Lord. For his sake I have suffered the loss of all things and count them as rubbish, in order that I may gain Christ**

Whispers Of A Butterfly Warrior

FAITH

Faith is what we all seem to look for and seek.
When life is very hard and things look very bleak.
It's when you realize your spouse is no longer your hero.
It is when the bank account balance suddenly is zero.
When your rent is due and the landlord won't bend.
When an addiction takes over your very good friend.
When you love someone and the love is not returned.
When you fail again after you thought you had learned.
Faith is what you have when all hope is at a loss.
It is a better day you seek after a fight with your boss.
It is the inner humble spirit teaching you to gently glide.
It is the courage you find when you really want to hide.
It is the stand you decided to take when no one else would.
It is the success you will make, when no one said you could.
It is God in your spirit, echoing for you to achieve.
When all you had in the world, was a dream to believe.
It is a conviction that God can and a hope that he will.
It is the impossible task that you somehow did full fill.
It is the faith you walked by when not using sight.
that led you out of darkness back into light

WHISPER

Do not run, be still, be quiet, be free and have no fear
When you don't know what to do God is whispering in your ear.
If you scream shout and yell, you will not be able to hear
That peace filled passive voice of God whispering in your ear

Do not get high, do not make that excuse to take that drink…
Be still for just a moment so that God can help you think
Do not ask people for advice, that does not help you hear
The truth is always heard when God is whispering in your ear

Don't look for love in sex, don't look for love in a friend…
The only love you find in people, is a love we call pretend
Don't get mad or sad because you think love made you shed tears
The only love you need to find is God whispering in your ear…

Don't call on your wife or husband, do not call on any man
Every time you do that, you step in the way of Gods real plan
Divine peace you cannot find in any person or any land….
When God whispers in your ear he will put peace in your hand.

Do not run from any situation, it will only come back worse…
It will come back stronger in strength as if it were a curse…
It will come back sideways, parallel, strait forward or reverse..
God sends things to teach us and sometimes heavily will disperse
God will whisper in your ear and your atonement will reimburse.

Philippians 1:20 As it is my eager expectation and hope that I will not be at all ashamed, but that with full courage now as always Christ will be honored in my body, whether by life or by death.

Philippians 1 :21 For to me to live is Christ, and to die is gain..

CHOOSE THE CROSS

I choose the cross, the nine inch nails, the crown of thorns on his blood drenched head,
The crucifix, the 6 hour journey and the tomb where he rose from the dead….
I choose the relationship with a King that has written in words everything to be said…
I choose the cross because every sin I have committed was washed in the blood he shed.

If we had a choice in the matter to go to hell or choose the cross….
So many of us, would be at the edge of a fire filled pit in a pity of loss.
Even the most religious people never experience a relationship with the boss.
His glory cannot reach you in your anger or pain and the loss of grace is the cost.

You can preach commandments to the people or poetry in the book of psalm.
But you cannot enter those gates unless you can feel that nail enter his palm.
You cannot walk on water like Peter unless Jesus makes your ocean calm.
You cannot feel, the weight of his forgiveness unless the devil unleashes a bomb.

Your addictions and pains may linger to your soul like a fierce lesion…
There will be choices to make and choosing against the savior is treason…
Your road to Damascus will be different than mine because your road has reason
Your cross and your journey will develop and overcome thru a different season…

There will be days GOD chooses to give you silence in your evolution….
He hears your prayers but makes you weigh thru the evilness of pollution…
He wants to see you stand on his word and your soul find thru him the solution
Because you know his promises and your faith will bring your life revolution.

I choose the cross, the nine inch nails, the crown of thorns on his blood drenched head,
The crucifix, the 6 hour journey and the tomb where he rose from the dead….
I choose the relationship with a King that has written in words everything to be said…
I choose the cross because every sin I have committed was washed in the blood he shed

**JOHN 14:16 Jesus said to him, "I am the way, and the truth, and the life. No one comes
to the Father except through me.**
**Revelation 21:4 He will wipe every tear from their eyes. There will be no more death or
mourning or crying or pain, for the old order of things has passed away.**

**1 John 2:2 He is the propitiation for our sins, and not for ours only but also for the sins
of the whole world.**

Christist Cries For You

Christ cries for you and weeps when you disobey his laws…
He is sorrowful when you do not love yourself even with your flaws
He still feels pain when a body is slain and weeps for the lost soul…
Even when it did not deserve, forgiveness to be made whole.

Christ cries for you when you abuse the gifts he gave so plush,
He weeps that you did not learn and bad choices made you rush…
You lost his vision and scrapped religion and ruined all you touch,
But his tears do fall and you hear his call even in a soft hush….

Christ cries for you when you compromise to treat others so badly…
He is sorrowful when he see's you corrupt your life so gladly,
He feels your pain when you say his name and hears you so sadly,
And he remains a constant in your life when you create the tragedy.

Christ cries when he see's peoples eyes focused on what satan buys
He is sorrowful when he see's you try but tangled by a web of lies..
He weeps for you when commandments break and excuses your reply,
Because when you sin against him, he is able to, give you another try.

His eyes well with tears when you choose the broken road….
He weeps for your soul when you hold onto the heavy load.
He is sorrowful that you did not hear all the words that he told.
Because he is the maker of your being and everything you hold.

Christ cries when chaos must teach them to listen and hear…
When your sinful self lingers to the world and you leer,
He weeps in your pain – he trembles when your in fear….
His sorrow becomes you so that you know he is here.

Isaiah 38:5 "Go, and say to Hezekiah, Thus saith the LORD, the God of David thy father, I have heard thy prayer, I have seen thy tears: behold, I will add unto thy days fifteen years."
2 Kings 20 :5 "Turn again, and tell Hezekiah the captain of my people, Thus saith the LORD, the God of David thy father, I have heard thy prayer, I have seen thy tears: behold, I will heal thee: on the third day thou shalt go up unto the house of the LORD."

THANK YOU

Thank you for sharpening me when you put the knife deep in my back
And gave me wounds so large that I could not force an evil response of a slap

Thank You for being so bitter and mean that you forced me down to crawl
And gave me the sting just like lightning that made Paul become Saul

Thank You for making me feel pathetic, weak, low in what you said to think
I confused you for a moral man who would not crap on me laughing as you drink

Thank You for being so disrespectful, telling me I was ugly in every way rude
And you still wanted to sleep with me because that's just a habit of a real dude

Thank You for being that girl who says she is my friend spreads gossip pretend
All about me because your jealous and envy was verbally attacking till you defend

Thank You for walking out of my life when I was laying on the floor crying
Because people who are fake make no mistake leave you when you are dying

Thank You for stealing and lying and stripping me while showing me your best
Because people can market themselves for a season but honor fails the long haul test

Thank You for giving me your opinion and telling me that I can't do it any better
Because I would have never known that I had grown beyond your personal vendetta

Thank You for saying I was pretty while you cheated, bringing women in my home
Because real men of GOD stand in a relationship of covenant even when they are alone

Thank You for negative denial of reality because you cannot face your demons within
And as I rewind all the time we spent together I see you suffocated me in your own sin

Thank You for refusing to speak to me when I offer an apology trying to correct
Your prideful bondage has no forgive or forget because your Ego is in such bad defect

Thank You for your criticism, weapons of arsenal words, and pushy negative view
Because I would have never known the preachers wife was really a devil in the pew

Thank you all those church people who chastised hatefully, my kind you did reject
Because now I can see the fruit of the tree was from GOD I need and not your respect

Thank You GOD for chasing me down and showing me love unconditional in length
And sending all these problems or situations as vehicles for me to lean on your strength.

YOUR GOD WILL

Your God will decapitate those mindsets and all of your very bad addictions,
Your God will bust down that self will that makes you choose such self affliction
Your God will be your strength when you are crying out because you have none
Your God will find you in your hiding place when there is no where left to run...
Your God will send Angels on your shoulder as he will touch you with hope divine
Your God will be in your heart and souls as only he can heal you in your mind
Your God will lead you and proceed you in safety by the will he has made for you
Your God will take away all the past that lashed and create your life full and new
Your God will be the love in our trouble and truth in what society taught and deceives
Your God will be the comfort to your lonely times because he stays and never leaves
Your God will be in your conscious, decision or reaction even when you wrongly choose
Your God will be the blessing of a new opportunity after you stumble and loose
Your God will be a feeling, a churn or inner guiding light that is unlimited in form
Your God will be the leading of your cynical self to die so that in Christ you are reborn
Your God will be in the faith that will lead and direct you correctly on how to proceed
Your God will be the courage in your dream lighting your path to be blessed and succeed

__ISAIAH 25:8__ Take courage in the knowledge that one day, there will be no more tears in our eyes. There will be no more sickness or sadness and no more death. " He will swallow up death in victory; and the LORD GOD will wipe away tears from off all faces"
__Romans 8:23__ And we know that all things work together for good to them that love God, to them who are the called according to his purpose.
__REVELATION 21:4__...And God shall wipe away all tears from their eyes; and there shall be no more death, neither sorrow, nor crying, neither shall there be any more pain: for the former things are passed away"

I take this Vow With GOD

I take this vow to love you and make a promise to GOD that I'll be
Joined to you in our spirits as an unbreakable covenant chord of three
To be faithful always, respectful, and next to you planted like a tree
To cherish you and honor GOD as we pray together on bended knee

I take this vow to love you with virtue like Jesus, as the Bible told
So we can lean on GOD together when the weight of the World is cold
I will be there in your sickness and health forever to have and to hold
Because I prayed everyday for you and believed GOD on a broken road

I take this vow to Love you, way beyond any time or any length
GOD is the rock of this union , always binding us in strength
I take this vow to love you, beyond the sun the moon and stars
GOD is the rock of our union, as his hands always holding ours

I take this vow to love you, thru the sunshine and the rain
To have our love unified by GOD, for we always will sustain
I take this vow to love you for rich or poor, in happiness and pain
GOD is the rock of our union, and a chord of three we will remain

I take this vow in front of GOD ,being Thankful he helped us thru
The kind of LOVE I search for, my best friend beyond far and few
I take this vow and covenant to promise my love genuine and true
GOD is the rock of this union, as he sees how much I love you….

I take this vow with GOD, I take this vow to always be
The kind of partner the bible, his spirit created inside of me
I take this vow with GOD, to protect you from any enemy
GOD is the rock of this union, and in him together we are free

I take this vow with you and GOD, as a symbol of our love
The kind of solid foundation only created from heaven above
I take this vow with you and GOD sealed in his faith and love
Till death may part us in earth and our souls bind in heaven above

HEBREWS 13:4 "Marriage must be respected by all, and the marriage bed kept undefiled, because God will judge immoral people and adulterers"

Everyday Grace

Everyday there are Angels among our closest friends,
We have an overflowing love from God that never ends.
Everyday there are crack heads trying to rehabilitate,
people sowed the seeds in the choices they make.
Everyday an abused woman is trying to leave her spouse,
but people emphasize the money car and house.
Everyday a child is looking for some love and attention.
but people in this world are lacking such affection.
Everyday we spend that money that reads 'In God We Trust',
but people kill each other for the power of money's lust.
Everyday we create energy in the words we speak and say,
instead of taking our feelings to God as we do pray.
Everyday a man dies at the hands of another man,
because we forget God can change things the way that he can.
Everyday we can be better than we chose the day before,
because God is at your side and he is knocking on your door.
Everyday we can help someone by just showing that we care,
because we know God is with us when life is not so fair.
Everyday we can elevate minds, of all those in need,
because Jesus elevated our souls as his hands began to bleed.

2 Corinthians 12:9 And he said unto me, My grace is sufficient for thee: for my strength is made perfect in weakness.

Jeremiah 29:10-12 For I know the plans I have for you,' declares the LORD, 'plans to prosper you and not to harm you, plans to give you hope and a future.

Don't Bow To Other Men

I will not be defined by your opinion of me or your distorted interpretation…
I cannot be molded or form fitted to become your greatest expectation,
A higher power guides my words and a war started with a thought and a pen,
I only work to make GOD smile and I do not bow to other men.

I have traveled the streets you would not go into, full of struggle and pain,
I have made excess money and had what you so desire, but all in vain.
Status made me into someone I could not look in the mirror, but you could train.
I conformed to it all and became a person who did not flinch at a body being slain,
Because, I had to meet the devil to know the great power of GOD's name.

God dragged me out of addiction with my hand holding onto the lies…
He taught me how to live honestly and my values cannot be compromised.
America sold me the same dream as you but you're the one who still buys..
We see death as a statistic as long as our company still thrives…
We forget he gave his own son in return for our lives.

Do you live for that dollar? Do you live for that dream?
Do you conform to be what they mold you to fit in the scheme?
Like the moon lights the earth-are you unique when you beam?
Are you someone else's muse-just silencing GODs dream?

I tell you the truth-you are in Babylon and a captive with no peace.
You try to please everyone except God-the most notorious disease…
You take you next breath toward death with such ease….
Because you want a status of the people that you try to please!
This is your moment-power only lies in the palm nailed to the wood of a tree!

I will not be defined by your opinion of me or your distorted interpretation…
I cannot be molded or form fitted to become your greatest expectation,
A higher power guides my words and a war started with a thought and a pen,
I only work to make GOD smile and I do not bow to other men.

Exodus 20:10 You shall not bow down to them or serve them, for I the Lord your God am a jealous God, visiting the iniquity of the fathers on the children to the third and the fourth generation of those who hate me,

Colossians 2:8 See to it that no one takes you captive by philosophy and empty deceit, according to human tradition, according to the elemental spirits of the world, and not according to Christ.

Woman Of Substance

A Woman of Substance is so unique and defined...
She carries herself upright and her words are refined.
She dares to be beauty by being subtle not bold..
A wife of noble character is worth more than rubies or gold.
Society teaches women that being provocative is some kind of virtue
When the Bible teaches that beauty is the gentle quiet spirit in you.
Your actions show your nobility, be careful how you choose...
How can you be a great mans asset if your worth nothing to loose.
Society teaches women to promote sex and wear less...
Yet integrity is more attractive than that little black dress.
When you learn intimacy is the softness of a hand to hand caress
Your virtue is an asset that will allow you to love and bless
A woman of substance needs no swing in her hip or skirt to her thigh,
she speaks stern in her belief and entices with a soft reply....
She needs not to expose with clothes beauty lives in her eye..
because she won't bend her Biblical law while other women try
and honesty lives thru her values not societies twisted lie.
Society teaches women that they only have power in being sexual,
Realize that by not using this weapon makes you more exceptional
The book of Proverbs says charm is deceptive and beauty is fleeting,
A woman only deceives her own worth by manipulating and cheating...
and she trades her soul for a heart that is bleeding...
when becoming a Woman of Substance was all she was needing.

PROVERBS 11:22.. "Like a gold ring in a pig's snout is a beautiful woman who shows no discretion."

PROVERBS 14:1 The wise woman builds her house, but with her own hands the foolish one tears hers down."

Whispers Of A Butterfly Warrior

The Ultimate Gift

The Ultimate gift for your soul, from just a baby in a manger…
Who came to take away your sin and keep you from the devils anger….
From the womb to the cross his mission was for you to be saved….
Salvation was the course that began on a dirt road of pain we paved

God's gift of Christmas day, when his only begotten son was birthed…
A messiah and martyr to redeem our flesh, of all who walk this earth
Three wise men knew that JESUS was his name before he staked his claim…..
and he had to walk in righteous ways when his destiny was to be slain….

He encountered the evil and was rebuked by the most prestige of men.
He never questioned his father or refused to be in the lions den…..
Humble and kind, never responding to those who tortured his skin…
For the purpose of his birth on Christmas was that he would take our sin.

The Ultimate gift of eternal life, given to you on Christmas day…..
With a crown of thorns and nine inch nails that would take his life away….
Joseph and Mary, simple minded people who protected the virgin womb
So that he could give you this Christmas gift, as he rose from death in a tomb.

The Ultimate gift he gave you in his birth was that you could be redeemed
And in his death he gave his blood that washed your sins and cleaned….
Rejoice in his birth that gave you life and resurrected you from hell….
The ultimate gift of beauty for the ashes you shift, was in the cross as it fell.

From water to wine a purpose so divine that we cannot rebuke our crime
Parting Oceans in a perfect line our Ultimate Gift surpasses space and time…..
And it was given to you in a manger on the dawn of Christmas day…..
The birth of our messiah, destined to die so he could take your sins away.

When GOD Makes You Bleed

When GOD makes you bleed, drains the life of your body so you will take heed,
Another Mountain will be moved for you and there is another planted seed…
Another Cross for you to bear as you learn another lesson of your moral creed,
Pain so overwhelming that you cannot bear to do another good deed…..

When GOD makes you bleed he will gut you to the bone like an apple to its core
You will be chastised, judged, rejected and ridiculed like the leopard or a whore…
You will find yourself all alone in a fetal position in the corner of the floor,
Because GOD needs all of your attention so that he can make you so much more.

GOD will make you bleed, cut precisely the vein drenching your black soul….
He will strip you of everything and self, so that he can make you better and whole.
Knife the skin covering you in darkness from the top of your head to your toe…
Bleed out your arsenal of weapons that self destruct your from your very goal.

GOD will make you bleed remorse slow, as patience has her way to your perfection…
You will feel the wrath as you find yourself in opposition by worldly human rejection,
But if you trade the process for progress then you will be faced with more correction,
You must be empty to feel the fullness of GODS abiding love and affection…
When GOD makes you bleed it is to guide you from hell to the path of right direction.

When GOD makes you bleed the devil will send demons to halt you in spiritual agitation,
For your chaos to be cosmos of stepping stones you must face the evil worldly aggravation,
This is your war to fight for the priceless privilege of your soul and its salvation…..
There will be bumps in the road as you bleed finding compelling relief in bad temptation,
Because God must destroy and rebuild making you into the image of his creation

When GOD makes you bleed it is because there is no way to get to the other side,
You can only go so far in self deception, that chooses to regret but then again lied…
You can move on from pain, hide in your pride and believe it is over after you cried,
But then you are back on that path of death that the world used against to misguide…..
A masterpiece cannot be made by GOD until every piece of your flesh has died.

I May Not Be.....

I may not be the person anyone thought that I would be
But GOD made provisions for all my beauty he could see
I may not be the person who follows all the biblical decree....
But GOD made forgiveness for people like me to become free

I may be jaded and wounded but my crooked paths are now strait
I may be unconventional and frustrated but on GOD I do now wait...

I may be sarcastic or drastic in truth but I will cut you till you bleed
And I know in my loss of you it was GOD's purpose of a need

I may be late for my appointments and sometimes forget to pay a bill
But I know how to heed when GOD tells me to stop and become still

I may not be the best boss or acquire status of fame you remember
And I know that at the end of my life all worldly things dismember

I may not be the person anyone thought that I would be
But GOD made provisions for all my beauty he could see
I may not be the person who follows all the biblical decree....
But GOD made forgiveness for people like me to become free

I may not be a preacher or have Gold Star Reviews upon my wall
But GOD decides how to use me to prevent others from that fall

I may not be the best mother and my house is sometimes unclean
And I know GOD gives me mercy when my mouth is sometimes mean

I may not be the role model you should use as any good example
But I know GOD picked me up when in the dirt I had been trampled

I may not be the type of woman who was ever High Society material
But I know that GOD does things to make you see the laws of spiritual

I may not be the person anyone thought that I would be
But GOD made provisions for all my beauty he could see
I may not be the person who follows all the biblical decree....
But GOD made forgiveness for people like me to become free

STIGMATA OF HIS LOVE

They say in Legends that the stigmata is the closes we get to the cross
The pain of the open wound in his hand and all of the blood loss…

The open flesh, cut deeply crest in the groove of his palm
The sacrifice that gave his life and made us read his poetic psalm

The Crown of thorns that repels the attack of evil horns…
The excruciating hours, of his cry, in whips of sin we mourn

The drops of liquid red for our soul to be fruitful and fed
The book of instruction, he left behind that so many people have read

The stigmata, a recreation of the tribulation he gave for our sin
The miles uphill with a cross on his back ,just so our faith could begin

The journey in the wilderness or the whip marks on his back
The fact that GOD gave his only son for human beings that are slack

The Stigmata, a very real invitation for others doubters to view
The rejection and reflection in the eyes of so many faithful innocent few

The burning bush or the water that he made into wine….
The fish replenished that fed thousands and the extra given time

The parted Ocean and the Blind man healed by just some spit
The very realization that we are not worthy but he will never quit

The wise man following Jesus and a plagued woman at a well
The creation of a place called heaven threatened by a fire pit in hell

The forgiveness, grace ,mercy, blessings and a baby in a manger
The stigmata of his love with promise that we treat like such a stranger

I FINALLY REALIZE....

I finally realize forgiveness is sometimes not given when needed
And life cannot be defined by the way society or people are treated
Spiritual Elevation only comes when everything else has defeated
But the hand of GOD is always waiting to say hello and be greeted

The pain you experience has purpose in his loving beautiful plan
And judgment means nothing if it comes from a sinful man…
People will perpetually hurt you just because they know they can
GOD blooms life of a flower with no force of growth to the land

I finally realize Redemption is found only when we have learned
And just when you think you want to give up the tides have turned
You may not think GOD heard you, but to love us, is all he yearned
And Grace is a favor that GOD has given and cannot be earned….

I finally realize forgiveness is sometimes not given when needed
And life cannot be defined by the way society or people are treated
Spiritual Elevation only comes when everything else has defeated
But the hand of GOD is always waiting to say hello and be greeted

Love is not a choice even when it causes us to hurt in heart
Meaning is defined by the finish of the race and not where you start
GOD allows the evil to come that sometimes may tear us apart…
Because he knows that disruption can cause a decision that is smart

I finally realize mistakes were meant to be used as a stepping stone
Walls and furniture build a house but only love can build a home…
If you fear what you have lost then you cannot see what is unknown
Because usually what has left your life was a pain you should not own

I finally realize forgiveness is sometimes not given when needed
And life cannot be defined by the way society or people are treated
Spiritual Elevation only comes when everything else has defeated
But the hand of GOD is always waiting to say hello and be greeted

Unspoken Invitation

You have an unspoken invitation and I am waiting for you, with open arms to greet….
There is room at my table and your name is already on a seat,
I will give you nourishment, and I will fill your hunger with food to eat.
I will surround you with abundance if you just take the chance to leap.
There is an unspoken invitation and a door wide open just for you,
There is a friend, a brother, a mate and I make you stronger by every two,
There is a fellowship and comfort, unconditional love so true…
There is a healing and a hope for your life to be made new
There will be learning and a teaching of my laws and the word,
There will be a presence of love that is felt but unheard.
There will be desire and hope in the friendship that has occurred.
There will be a vision that is clear in what the world has blurred.
There will be atonement and forgiveness for your worst sin,
I will burn it to ashes and lock it away in a tin…
You will be cleansed by my blood that overflows from the rim.
You will be given a purpose for my work that you must begin.
You are invited to my table where you will find peace and grace.
There is a seat with your name and I've prepared a special place.
You're a garment of beauty that only I could create…
There are only good things for my children so why do you wait

1 PETER 4:13 But even if you should suffer for what is right, you are blessed. "Do not fear what they fear ; do not be frightened…

EZRA 10:4 Rise up; this matter is in your hands. We will support you, so take courage and do it.

The Package

You can have many great options but decide you are always waiting for perfection
And so you resent your life because the package didn't fit in your wishes reflection
And so you prayed with no delay but still couldn't feel all of GOD'S devoted affection
Because the greatest gift GOD sent was a package you told yourself wasn't a selection
And so you open all the wrapping and unravel everything but the one worth the mention
Because you had your mind closed so tight GODS package received no attention......

People always tell me all the time that maybe they must have missed the blessing boat
Like all those Christians who preach to a congregation but inside lost compassion or hope
They have mental imagery of perfection, reach out for an ore of life or hang to any rope
But the beautiful miracle they received from GOD was a package that didn't make them gloat

Upset and sad looking at expectations of what in life you missed and how long is the road
Busy making adjustments ,changes or requirements to become something better were told…
Expecting a picture or a vision of the very perfect gifts as things you wish you can hold
And so you missed the blessing GOD sent you because his package didn't fit that kind of mold.

If you expect love to be unfolded but only a certain way with no barriers to ever jump,
And if you think a smooth road of wealth or success exist and there is no financial slump…
The perfect spouse should smile and inspire but never have attitude or be a grump
And that job is one where there is less work to grind but you get a promotional bump
Well then every beautiful package that GOD sent was what you viewed as trash to dump.

You see that people are so busy making plans they never see how life happens beautifully
They are busy waiting on a flower to sprout but GOD gave them this amazing Strong tree
But they were intending in their own mind exactly what they wanted that they never did see
The package was perfect and in front of them but it wasn't what they thought it would be

You can fall in love with someone who equals you but they were not what you expect
So instead of allowing the gift of love you push it away to later hurt in painful regret
You can be given great opportunity to excel or advance and somehow refuse to let….
The favor that was sent your way because it was not the vision you wanted to accept.

You can have many great options but decide you are always waiting for perfection
And so you resent your life because the package didn't fit in your wishes reflection
And so you prayed with no delay but still couldn't feel all of GOD'S devoted affection
Because the greatest gift GOD sent was a package you told yourself wasn't a selection
And so you open all the wrapping and unravel everything but the one worth the mention
Because you had your mind closed so tight GODS package received no attention......

BUTTERFLY WARRIOR'S WHISPER

Butterfly Warriors Whisper when there is no light left on Damascus Road
They hold on when burned by lightning to all the promises GOD foretold
Butterfly Warriors Whisper when you have nothing in this life to behold
Because your power breaks the stronghold, and thru Christ you will uphold

Butterfly Warrior, let me glide on your beautiful soft elegant wing
Let me hear you whisper all the words, GOD wants me to sing
Butterfly Warrior give me strength to say the very needed thing
And guide me, to give peaceful promise of what recovery may bring

Let me show the world that the anguish can be relinquished
Whisper softly GOD'S conquering element that it will be finished
I am liquefied like a butterfly and beautified by what they tarnished
And recovery is only found inside a warrior who can be harnessed

Lead them out of the fire filled pit by the power held inside
Teach them no weapon formed against them shall ever abide
Give them my vulnerable flesh, that other people always want to hide
So they know the transformation road is one where you have died

Butterfly Warriors Whisper when there is no light left on Damascus Road
They hold on when burned by lightning to all the promises GOD foretold
Butterfly Warriors Whisper when you have nothing in this life to behold
Because your power breaks the stronghold, and thru Christ you will uphold

Stretch and magnify to all those souls being courageously liquefied
Let them know they are not alone and so many others never even tried
Show them what they leave behind will bring them relief as they cried
But only a true warrior makes decisions from an inner fighting guide

And when they tell you that all hope is lost, every resource been exhausted
Believe nothing that people bring to you because it is always distorted
The true words in the book of life can always be seen and recorded
But the Warrior can never whisper if the mission of a butterfly is aborted

Genuine and unique never changing for any human acceptance
Believing in your formation that was whispered in your repentance
A butterfly Warrior gets its reward in every beautiful human reflectance
And your success to soar, fly and conquer is GOD'S rightful vengeance

Butterfly Warriors Whisper when there is no light left on Damascus Road
They hold on when burned by lightning to all the promises GOD foretold
Butterfly Warriors Whisper when you have nothing in this life to behold
Because your power breaks the stronghold, and thru Christ you will uphold

For It Is I

For it is I who loved you in times of tribulation..
For it is I who revealed all truths in speculation
For it is I who gave you love, courage and inspiration
For it was I who created the world in raw animation…

For it was I who gave, receiving nothing with no appreciation
For it was I who shined on you and had no expectation
For it was I who struggled for you in the act of deprivation…

For it was I who took weakness and fear, returning your strength
For it was I who will not judge, to love beyond any length

For it was I who cradled you from dusk, till dawn
For it is I who battled fire in hell and stayed almighty strong.
For it is I who will come back for those believers who belong.

For it is I who created your very own skin….
For it is I who gave my sons life for all the worlds sin.
For it was I who was nailed hands and feet to the cross
For it is I who bled, so your soul would not be at a loss

For it is I who shed blood seven times before conquering calvery
For it is I who hath made, men of blindness see…
For it is I who took you from bondage and made you free

For it is I who hath the power to heal and make the handicap walk
For it is I who make you function to move think and talk

For it is I who made you from dust crafting your hands, legs and ears
For it is I who made you capable and gave you grace amongst you peers
For it is I who gives you courage against the demonic powers you fear
For it is I from birth to death, watching you and giving grace thru every year

For it is I who will return and it is my people I will retrieve….
For it is I who will be waiting for the ones who do believe…
Sins, Destruction and struggle will envelope the world behind I leave…
Why are you still waiting why do you still become deceived….

For it is I ….it is I who is waiting on your reply….
You still have not come to me …again I ask you why?

<u>Revelation 3:20,</u>

Here I am! I stand at the door and knock. If anyone hears my voice and opens the door, I will come in and eat with him, and he with me.

Acknowledgements:

My Savior: Jesus Christ

Thank You GOD, My Heavenly Father who is almighty and loved me enough to send his son to the cross for my sins. Thank You for my gift of poetic talent, providing a unique ability to be used for your purpose. Thank You LORD, for allowing me to experience the trials and tribulations that developed me into a person who does not hide behind my past faults but who has become brave enough to embrace and share every detail of those circumstances, so that someone else can benefit to find your love, mercy, grace and forgiveness that is unconditional. I am your bondservant- Thank You for salvation!!!

My Mother: Beverly Hawkinson

Thank You for always challenging me and understanding. For being the prayer warrior, that kept me alive and connected to the power of GOD in my worst times. I love you Always. I will someday be the daughter that breaks every generational curse by being a woman to be used by GOD, powerful and mighty in faith. One day you will understand the purpose of your tears and the pain that I caused you may someday heal. There are no words to express how sorry I am for the rough years that has hindered a great relationship and bond. Maybe someday you will find the ability to heal and let go of the past that keeps you in bondage. The saddest part of my journey will be that you really don't know me for the person I have become in this lifetime but as I move forward I understand that GOD will always leave my past behind me and have a place at his table when my family, acquaintances or friends do not, because GOD forgave me and I finally forgave myself for the road less traveled.

My Sons, Aaron & Isaiah

You are my reason for living and GOD lent you to me to guide you in your life path. Parts of my journey you endured and watched for the knowledge gained in your smalls souls that will become huge conquering spirits .May you guide with compassion and strength that endures every trial. Remember the greatest achievement in life is to make GOD smile and if you live that way abundance and blessings will live inside of you. I love you always and limitless in this world and in heaven. The "Simple Man" receives the best things in life if he follows GOD's word and not people, Remember everyday how much I love you and that my love goes with you on your journey as adults in Christ, Remember self sacrifice is always seen by GOD and he judges your heart and deeds daily, We create the end result no matter where we start in life or what comes against us because GOD is always with us in our spirit. I love you and everything I have done is to redeem what I could not do in your early years.

Robin Bristow

You are closer than a sister and the one person who never left my side when everyone else did. Your faith in me is incredible and has helped carry me when I wanted to give up on my dream. You are my family in every way, one who showed me unconditional love in friendship and believed in me when I lacked the faith in myself to move forward. Thank You for pushing me like no one else did and allowing me to be myself and loving me for who I am when everyone in my life put limitations on my strength and endurance to succeed and overcome. Our relationship has spanned many triumphs ,trials ,pains, losses and distance but never lacked love, compassion or dependability to move forward in our journey of life .No journey in miles has ever changed that bond of friendship or loyalty like family that we have with each other. Thank You for being someone in my life that would drive all night to get to me and be there in my most excruciating moments. There are absolutely no words to express the how much I appreciate and love you. Thank You, may we have many more days of laughter and grace together .You are my best friend even on the days we don't like what each other chooses we somehow learn to adapt in an unconditional acceptance and understanding that many people never find in friends .Thank You!

Mark Adams

When most Christians wanted to mold me you gave me friendship. Thank you for helping me, when I had forgotten how to accept grace. For being a spiritual mentor that would allow me to tell the truth and made me realize that I was always trying to make GOD love me when he already did. I am inspired by your journey and the ability to see my weakness of thinking I had to earn or "deserve" my blessings that were promised…..thank you for those days you prayed for me and listened to my spiritual struggle with pure compassion and no judgment that allowed me to show my vulnerability because I lacked trust in people. I will always hold the "Ragamuffin Gospel" as a tool and thank you for reminding me how God loves the ragamuffin just like me. Thank You

April Davis

You are the person I sat and talked to every Saturday night for almost two years. Thank You for being my friend and keeping me grounded. Those conversations helped break the temptation to return to my old lifestyle and helped me get to the other side of the mountain when every odd was stacked against me to fail. You have been a great support as a friend and those nights made me learn how to be still and at peace in my lonely suffering. I now enjoy my silence and know who I am instead of what everyone wanted me to be because of it. You are my "people" and a beautiful soul that has helped lighten the load with conversation. THANK YOU!

Angel Turner

The person who told me, that "I am the exception and not the rule". Thank You for seeing me in ways that I could not see myself at times and for entering spiritual talks in regard to relationships and life that a lot of female friends could not comprehend. Your ability to see what I was striving to do and supporting me in my efforts has had a great positive impact on helping me to keep pushing forward and your support has been endless. Thank You for always pushing me to get the better part of myself and see the people around me who were not willing to go the extra mile that a real friendship takes at some bumps in the road. Thank You

Mickey Turner

I am proud to know you and amazed at all the strives you have made spiritually as a man of GOD in a business world, it is rare and a true gem that stands out in a cut throat dog eat dog world and I admire the way you have evolved in your walk with Christ and embraced changes to be a better version of yourself when so many others just pass that mark as a road they rather not endure. I will always remember your dating advice because I did listen even if I did not use it and usually you were correct. I am glad to say My friend has a great husband who searches and stepped up to find GOD… blessings for your family always, Thank You

Amanda Galloway

You are my favorite country girl, and the laughter we had every day for two years despite all the struggles in life is not replaceable. Thank You for the listening without judgment and the ability to make light of a lot of things that weighed me down or disturbed my soul. The long texts and being someone who I could go to when so many people were stretching me thin .I love you girl and know our friendship will remain many years to come Thank You!!

Dawn & Ted Mc Pheeters

You have the hearts of gold and GOD knows every stray person you have given shelter to and fed. Thank you for the peaceful days on the boat and the couch when I had nowhere to go in the middle of the night. I believe you have no idea how your compassion has really touched other people's lives or made a difference. I hope somewhere that I left my fingerprint on your life also in a positive way. May GOD always bless you and your family for the support and unconditional love you give to others. Thank You

Susan Tollivero

I never saw you coming and GOD surprised me with a great mentor who had the ability to stretch me even when I was uncomfortable in my own skin, You saw the ability that so many people chose to leave in a complacent place. Thank You for being that boss who knew I could do more and become more if I was challenged. I will always remember the lesson of learning that criticism is a tool for advancement and constructive if it is received by a person as a stepping stone to become better. The wisdom I have acquired in knowing you has been priceless in my journey, spiritually and professionally. I will never forget that you made every effort to help me evolve and become more for my children Thank You!

Robert Todd

Thank You for being a man who lives correctly and seeks the heart of GOD. You make me want to be a better person. You stopped your day to pray with me when not many people thought I was worth the prayer .I will always remember that and how much it meant to me when the thought GOD had forgotten me and the faith I had was fading away. It made a huge difference in my walk with GOD and my view of Christian men. You have no idea how much I respect and admire the faithful strive you make to be a man of nobility, character, and humility. You have crossed my path in life for many years and who you have become in GOD has made a great impact on me to keep strong in faith and I am sure you will cross my path again, hopefully I can make that difference to someone else in this life ,

Julie Mc Gorty

There is nothing I could say to describe how awesome you are as a person and the best version of you is yet to come. I remember when I thought I had failed you as a friend in your walk and road but you got it just the way GOD wanted you to. You are a living testament that people can beautifully transform every negative to a positive.. You will forever be an inspiration to lives even if you are not told or rewarded but in what you embraced, faced down and overcame. Your personal strength is an attribute nobody can ever take from you and it will remain a force in GOD that will be magnified by his light as you move forward. You are a success in every way defying all obstacles that many people never face in their life. I love you and support you and am proud to know such a great, inspiring and graceful human being. Remember that GOD never consults your past to determine your future and live in the endless possibility of all GOD's promises to renew and restore. Thank You

Judy Gossett

I know that anytime day or night I can pick up a phone and you will give me compassion, unconditional love and support like no one else ever has. Instantly you became a mother figure in my life as well as a friend, In every flaw I exhibit, you accepted me with open arms and always pointed out my strengths and talents. You never changed who you are in this life to prove how much you love GOD to anyone and that is something I do not see often enough and so respect with admiration. Our spiritual and unconditional hearts do have a place where they can be embraced and not tortured by the human effect of this world and that place will always be in GOD's kingdom. You are my family in every way and covenant in the spirit can be thicker than any blood bond on Earth. I thank GOD every day that he brought you in my life to be a motivating loving force I needed so desperately. Thank You!